BASICS FOR BUYERS
A Practical Guide
to Better Purchasing

SOMERBY R. DOWST

Managing Editor
PURCHASING Magazine

Sponsoring Editor: Walter E. Willets

CBI PUBLISHING COMPANY, INC.
51 Sleeper Street, Boston, Massachusetts 02210

For My Nephew
Martin William Souders II
1st Lt., U.S.A.F.
1942–1967

Printing(last digit): 13 12   11 10

International Standard Book Number: 0-8436-1301-7
Library of Congress Catalog Card Number: 74–156479
Copyright © 1971 by Cahners Publishing Company, Inc.
Printed in the United States of America.

CONTENTS

PART FOUR   SUPPLIER RELATIONS

PART FIVE   TRAINING AND SELF–DEVELOPMENT

PREFACE

Over the years, and especially during the last decade or so, many excellent books on purchasing have been published. To a great extent, the stepped-up tempo of publication reflects the increased recognition that the purchasing function has gained: from top management, from the academic community, from other professions, and from the public at large.

This recognition, in turn, stems from the realization that purchasing is not merely a clerical operation, but a vital and dynamic part of any enterprise that has to buy materials, equipment, supplies or services.

In the typical manufacturing company, for example, the purchasing department spends an amount equal to 52% of the annual sales dollar. In process industries where labor/material cost ratios are traditionally low, the percentage is even higher. This means that purchasing has an unparalleled opportunity to improve profits by reducing costs.

Or, in non-profit organizations such as hospitals, schools and government agencies, skillful buying by the purchasing department will result in additional funds being available to upgrade the quality of patient care, student education, or governmental service for each tax dollar.

Against this background, it's not surprising that an increasing number of colleges and universities are offering full-credit courses in purchasing, and that the literature on the subject is constantly expanding.

Almost without exception, however, the existing textbooks on purchasing are directed either at students of general business administration (to give them an overview of purchasing's position vis-à-vis marketing, production, etc.), or at purchasing agents and managers (to present a comprehensive rundown on the principles and policies of industrial procurement).

The purpose of this book is a little different.

It is, primarily, a book for buyers—a practical handbook for the men and women who work under the supervision of a department manager, to get the right goods in at the right time at the right price.

Since it is not meant to be a textbook *per se,* its main value to other (non-buyer) readers will probably be to give business students an insight into the practical problems facing on-the-line buyers—or to help new-to-purchasing executives in smaller firms develop workable procedures.

The book had its genesis as a series of articles which the author wrote for *Purchasing* magazine. In its present form, about half of its chapters are slightly revised and updated versions of those articles. The other chapters are new—having been added to give a complete picture of the purchasing function from the line-buyer's viewpoint.

The author hopes that the book will be of value to those in the buying position—by suggesting ways in which the typical problems of day-to-day buying can most efficiently be met. For, while the top purchasing executive in any organization may set policies and overall procedures, it's essentially up to the buyer to turn policies and procedures into action.

S.R.D.

ACKNOWLEDGMENTS

The author gratefully acknowledges the assistance of the following purchasing executives and their companies, in permitting him to use various purchasing forms as illustrations in this book:

Mr. Charles Adams, Wright Line, Division of Barry Wright Corporation; Mr. Conrad Disabato, General Binding Corporation; Mr. Robert Druva, Stearns-Roger Corporation; Mr. John Grunewald, Duncan Electronics, Inc.; Mr. V. R. Nelson, Champion Dish Washing Machine Company; Mr. Harry Rosen, Xerox Data Systems; and Mr. Walt Sattler, The Upjohn Co.

Of the other forms illustrations in the book, some have been designed by the author—to suggest systems ideas that may assist the reader in developing forms keyed to his own daily buying routines.

In other cases, the forms illustrated have been taken from the author's files, which have been built up during hundreds of interviews with purchasing agents and buyers. These interviews were conducted in connection with the author's position as an editor for *Purchasing* magazine—but some of the forms collected do not indicate the companies in which they are used. The author regrets, therefore, that due credit for these forms cannot be given to companies or individuals.

Along the same lines, the author would also like to thank all the purchasing executives and buyers whom he has interviewed over the past nine years, for so freely communicating their ideas on how the buying job can best be handled.

If this book is successful as a basic guide *for* buyers, the success will be due in no small measure to the fact that it is also a book *by* buyers.

PART ONE

The Basic Purchasing Cycle

Whether you call it the "purchasing cycle" or the "accounts payable routine," procurement is one of the two basic systems that are common to any business. The other is the sales/marketing or accounts receivable routine. The two are interdependent in two ways.

In the first place, obviously, a buying company's purchasing cycle is what kicks off the sales routine for each of its suppliers. The customer sends a purchase order, and the supplier either ships from stock or enters a production order in his plant. Then, after shipping the goods, the supplier sends the customer a bill and the customer issues a check as payment.

This is why marketing men have claimed for years that "nothing happens until somebody sells something"—with purchasing professionals quickly retorting that "nothing happens until somebody buys something."

In the second place, and perhaps not quite so obviously, purchasing is related to sales *within* each company. Costs of raw materials are directly reflected in end product selling prices, delivery delays on inbound shipments can raise havoc with outbound schedules, and lack of a spare part for a production machine can also scramble the carefully planned timetables for customers' orders.

Or, if a company doesn't buy parts and components of adequate quality, the result can be a black eye from which it may take marketing years to recover.

Since any effort to make purchasing more effective should start with an understanding of what's involved in the basic procurement cycle, let's look at the steps that are involved in chronological order.

In its simplest state, the buying process starts with recognition of a need—either by the stockroom or an individual requisitioner.

It next proceeds to selection of a supplier to fill that need.

Finally, the buyer and the supplier come to an agreement on how and when the vendor will perform to fill the need.

As later sections of this book will discuss in more detail, the buyer's over-all responsibility doesn't end when he issues a purchase order. But for practical purposes the three steps noted above represent the key activities every buyer must be concerned with day in and day out.

The chapters in this section, therefore, are designed to pinpoint ways in which the buyer can most effectively handle these basic tasks—with particular emphasis on ways in which already established procedures can possibly be refined and polished.

1

STOCK CONTROL AND INVENTORY RECORDS

A buyer's role in inventory control will vary considerably, depending on his company's organizational theories and policies.

In some firms, the buyer himself may be directly responsible for keeping track of stock records and establishing order points and quantities on the items he purchases.

In other companies, there may be a materials management set-up under which both purchasing and inventory control (along with production planners) report to the same department head.

In most firms, however, the buyer's inventory control responsibility is less direct and formal. A separate stock-keeping group watchdogs receipts and disbursements—and sends the buyer the requisitions that trigger replenishment orders.

The systems that the stock-keeping group uses to control inventory, similarly, can range all the way from the simplest procedures to highly sophisticated plans and programs. One company's inventory policies may be aimed at keeping no more than 120 days' supply of any item on hand at any time; another firm may use complex mathematical formulas to determine economic order points and quantities.

One of the most popular EOQ (economic order quantity) formulas, for example, is known as the square root formula:

$$Q = \sqrt{\frac{2\,RS}{IC}}$$

In this formula, Q is the economic order quantity; R is annual usage; S is the cost of issuing a purchase order; I is inventory-carrying cost as a percent of inventory value; and C is unit cost of the part in question.

As a buyer, you don't necessarily have to know the mathematics involved in deriving such formulas. But, no matter what systems the inventory control specialist uses at his end of the procurement cycle, you have to work closely with him for maximum buying efficiency.

If you do coordinate your buying activities with the stock-keeping and inventory control staffers, both you and they will benefit in many ways:

1. Working together, you and the inventory control group can develop an A-B-C analysis of the items you buy.

An A-B-C analysis is simply a determination of the relative ratios between the number and the dollar values of the items you purchase repetitively for stock. Quite typically it will show that 5% of the items (the "A" goods) account for 75% of the dollars; 25% of the items (the "B" goods) account for 20% of the dollars; and 70% of the items (the "C" goods) account for 5% of the dollars.

(An A-B-C analysis, in fact, is a classic example of what is known as "Pareto's Law." Vilfredo Pareto was an Italian economist and sociologist, who died in 1923. He first propounded the theory that, in any type of activity, a small percentage of forces will influence a large percentage of results. Or, as one observer has put it, that 20% of the girls on any street will generate 80% of the whistles.)

The main purpose of an A-B-C analysis of inventoried goods is to pinpoint the high-dollar "A" items on which you and the inventory control group should concentrate your respective efforts. These are the parts or materials where you will want to focus your cost-reduction efforts for maximum payoff; they are also the ones where inventory-turnover goals should be considerably higher than those for "B" or "C" goods.

It may be that your company has already run an A-B-C analysis across-the-board on all its purchased items. Or, you may be a commodity specialist buying just one major material, such as steel. But it will almost always pay off to run such a study on the specific items you're responsible for. You can set up subcategories, such as type or shape of material, in classifying your buys. As a steel buyer, for example, you might find that most of your dollars are accounted for by rod, strip, coil or what-have-you.

2. Inventory-turnover in general is another area where your buying efforts can give a big assist to the inventory control crew. This is important because inventory-carrying costs (the "I" in the square root formula) run as high as 25% to 30% in some companies.

Such costs include obsolescence, theft and other physical loss; space charges for storage; labor charges for handling; insurance fees; the cost of money which could otherwise be invested somewhere else; and, in some states, personal property taxes.

The rate of inventory-carrying costs varies from firm to firm depending on many factors: how susceptible goods are to pilferage or obsolescence; how easy or difficult they are to store and handle; etc. But the important thing is that it takes action by the buyer to reduce these costs.

Every time you convince a supplier to make and hold goods, for example, you're making a direct contribution to company profits. And the same holds true for your successful efforts to prevent supplier over-runs, over-shipments or early deliveries.

3. Concerted action by the buyer and the inventory control group can also alleviate the small order problem that plagues buyers (and sellers) in all lines of business.

Reason: One of the best ways to eliminate small orders is to turn them into big ones. If you can get the stock-keeping staff to cooperate by pooling requirements for similar items, you'll find yourself receiving fewer requisitions for more items.

In addition to the paperwork and clerical savings resulting from such ganged orders, you'll probably find that unit prices also drop, thanks to volume discounts.

4. The stockroom's records, which provide a comprehensive rundown on receipts and disbursements, usually give more detailed information on an item than purchasing's commodity-history cards do. Example: year-to-date figures on disbursements, by month.

You can often use this data on usage trends in determining what items are suitable for long-term contracts, and what types of long-range agreement would be best. And, if you're shooting for a "stockless purchasing" plan, under which the supplier will fill individual requisitioners' needs direct, you *have* to have this data to present to prospective sources.

5. Standardization programs also require close buyer liaison with

PART NO.	DESCRIPTION									
USED ON	INV. CLASS.	STD. PKG.	RUNS WITH	WT.	COMM. CODE	S/R LOCATION	U/M	MIN. / MAX.	LEADTIME	

DATE	REF.	IN	OUT	BAL	DATE	REF.	IN	OUT	BAL.
J									
F									
M									
A									
M									
J									
J									
A									
S									
O									
N									
D									

Fig. 1 Stock record card, the inventory control group's prime reference, is ordinarily maintained outside of purchasing department. But it's the buyer's responsibility to see that basic information on packaging and lead times is always up to date and accurate.

the inventory control department. A "standard," by definition, is an item or group of items that's used by one or more individuals in a company for a specific purpose or purposes. All stocked items are therefore candidates for standardization—and a successful standards program will lower prices, reduce order-frequency, and free storage space in the stockroom for other uses.

However, for any of these five or other benefits to become a reality rather than wishful thinking, there is specific data that you must transmit to the inventory control man *because you are his only source for it.* Such information includes:

(a) Normal lead times
(b) Standard packaging quantities
(c) Volume discounts and price-break levels
(d) Odd-lot or broken-package surcharges
(e) Combination-order possibilities
(f) Impending price changes
(g) Tooling or set-up requirements

The inventory controller doesn't have to have all this data on all the items he handles—except for (a) and (b), which are always required. But there will be many occasions when you'll want to go back at him and suggest boosting requisition quantities to take advantage of a volume discount or to beat an upcoming price increase.

Or, if you're thinking of switching to a new source that will require extra lead time to prepare tooling, you'd better let the inventory control group know about it well in advance of actual reorder time.

Fig. 1 shows a typical stock record card that an inventory control staff might use in keeping track of all the parts and materials it's responsible for. Whether or not you have any say in the design of such a record, you've got to remember that it's the inventory control man's prime reference. It's his Bible—but it will be only as useful to him as you can make it.

Since lead time data and other basic information change from time to time, it's up to you to see to it that the reference material on the stock record card is always up to date and accurate. That's the very first step toward effective buying of the repetitive items that account for the big purchasing dollars.

2

THE PURCHASE REQUISITION

A purchase requisition is the prime input that starts things rolling in the procurement cycle.

It may be a request to replenish stock on a repetitive item.

It may be a one-time request for a particular product or service.

But, whatever the requisition calls for, it represents an unfilled requirement of some sort within the buyer's company. And, just as the buyer's job makes him *responsible* for servicing such needs, receipt of a particular requisition gives him the *authority* for each specific purchase. At the same time, it makes him *accountable* for filling the need within whatever purchasing policies and procedures his company has developed.

So, while a buyer's incoming mail usually consists of a broad range of communications—everything from suppliers' advertising circulars to internal reports and memos on general subjects—it's the daily purchase requisitions that should get his top-priority attention.

This is a matter of self-protection as much as anything else. Some urgent requisitions may be hand-delivered with specific comments highlighting their rush nature. But others may come to the buyer through normal channels as though there were nothing extraordinary at all about their requested delivery dates. (In many cases involving one-time purchases, in fact, the requisitioner may be completely unaware that he's being less than realistic when he specifies a near-impossible "date wanted.")

The first step in processing requisitions, then, should be to identify those that require fast attention—and to establish at least a tentative timetable for handling them. This is essentially a matter of judgment, based on many factors in addition to the delivery date on the requisition.

Suppose, for example, that a buyer receives two requisitions at 9:00 A.M.—one calling for next-day delivery of an off-the-shelf local distributor's item, the other requesting three-week delivery of a custom-made part.

If the custom-made part normally takes four weeks to produce, and if the buyer knows that an afternoon phone call to the distributor will easily get the stock item to the receiving dock within 24 hours, his course of action is clear. He should first get the custom job into the works—sandwiching in a call to the local distributor as early as possible before closing time.

This is an extreme example, of course. But it illustrates how the buying job demands not only a service-oriented viewpoint (to handle the tough requisitions along with the easy ones, and to get the goods in when they're needed), but also the ability to make fast decisions that are more than snap judgments.

For that matter, when a buyer receives any requisition, he's immediately put into a position where he has to exercise two levels of judgment—each of which highlights one aspect of his two-sided job. One level is mechanical in nature, focusing on the procedural details of turning requisitions into purchase orders. The other level is creative, centering on ways and means to make each purchase the best one possible for the company.

Today, with the emphasis on purchasing's potential contribution to profit, it's fashionable to stress the second level. In cold fact, however, it is impossible for a buyer to use level-two judgment until he has mastered the basics of level one. It's just as ridiculous to stigmatize a man as an "order placer" simply because he knows how to place an order, as it is to call him a "good buyer" if he never proceeds to level-two creative type work.

With this proviso in mind, let's look at the more elemental steps in processing a requisition. While some of these steps may be handled by a clerical section or service group in large purchasing departments, they're still important parts of the buying process. Here are the points that have to be queried on most if not all requisitions:

1. *Type of form.* Some companies use different requisition forms for different types of requirement. Is the form the correct one for the items it covers?

2. *Approval.* Does the individual signing the form have authority to approve requisitions? Does his signature match purchasing's signature card, if there is such a by-the-book control?

3. *Account number.* Is the account number to be charged the correct one? Is the approver authorized to charge that account? (In some companies, accounting may check this out after the p.o. has been written.)

4. *Date wanted.* Does the delivery date allow enough lead time for normal p.o. processing by purchasing, and order handling by the supplier? Is it expressed as a firm date? If it merely says "Rush," "Soonest," or "A.S.A.P. (as soon as possible)," what does the requisitioner really mean? Will he accept supplier's overtime charges or premium transportation such as air express?

5. *Quantity.* Does the quantity requested clearly identify measurable units such as pieces, pounds, gallons, feet, etc.? How does it compare with the "amount on hand" entry if there is one?

6. *Description.* Are specifications complete and detailed? Will the supplier understand them if they're transcribed verbatim to the purchase order? Or should the buyer edit them to make them conform to commercial terminology?

7. *Ship to.* Is the shipment to be delivered to a location other than the buying company's plant or offices—such as orders for outside processing on materials? If so, how will the receiving paperwork be handled?

8. *Dollar value.* Will the size of the order make written quotations mandatory under the company's purchasing policies? Is the approver authorized for the dollar value? Can the buyer award the order without an O.K. from his supervisor? How far up the purchasing chain of command will approvals be necessary?

9. *Supplier's name.* If the requisitioner has entered a supplier's name on the requisition, is he merely trying to be helpful by suggesting a possible source? Or is he guilty of back-door buying, having already said or implied that the vendor is assured of the order?

These nine points cover items which have to be queried on incoming requisitions, before the buyer even picks up a pencil to work them over. But there are also at least six additional questions that the buyer has to ask himself as he annotates each requisition for the order typist. Here they are:

10. *Supplier's name/address.* Can the supplier's processing of the order be speeded up by addressing it to the attention of a specific indi-

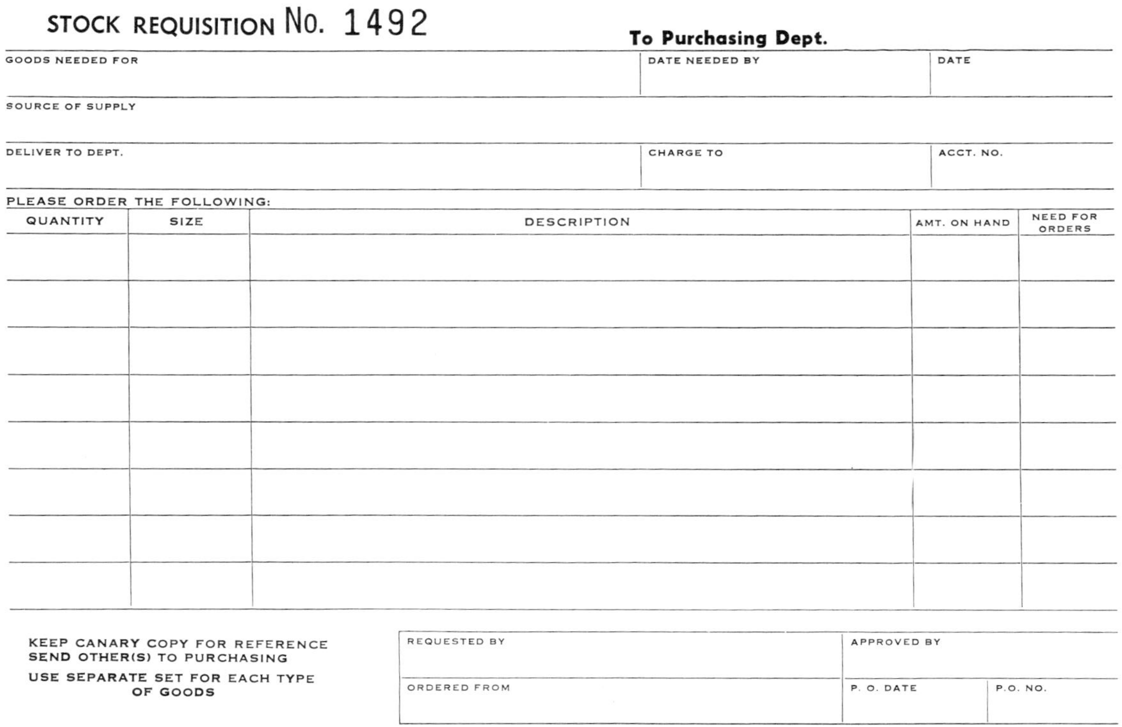

Fig 2. Stock requisition forms like this one are used by many companies; other firms, especially the larger ones, design custom forms to meet their particular needs. Regardless of the forms used, however, there are specific questions that a buyer must check out whenever a requisition hits his desk.

vidual in his company? (This is especially important in dealing with head-quarters offices of large firms.)

11. *Delivery date.* Will the delivery date satisfy the requisitioner? Has the supplier been realistic in promising it, or is he just hoping that "things will work out O.K. somehow"?

12. *F.o.b. point.* On f.o.b. shipping point orders, is there a chance of getting the supplier to "equalize" his freight charges to meet those of a closer competitor? On f.o.b. destination orders, will the supplier provide inside delivery?

13. *Ship via.* Are the transportation modes and carriers specified the best ones for the order? Are there any special problems such as weather or strikes to consider? Has the traffic department checked out such situations?

14. *Terms of payment.* Are the supplier's terms of payment satisfactory from an administrative as well as a financial angle? For example, do they permit the accounting department to pay invoices monthly or semi-monthly without forfeiting cash discounts?

15. *Price.* Are one-time costs such as tooling and set-up charges clearly identified as such? Is the price entry expressed in the same units of measurement as the quantity entry?

In industry and business today, there are undoubtedly hundreds of thousands of types of purchase requisition in use—differing in size, style, number of parts, number and variety of headings, etc. They range all the way from stock forms like the one illustrated in Fig. 2, to computerized printouts that include data on former purchases, usage trends, and current bid information.

But, no matter what type of form a company uses, every requisition is a request for service from the purchasing department. It's a requirement that the buyer must attend to in some way, even if he doesn't fill it exactly as specified.

When a buyer begins to question requisitions from other angles—specifications, materials, tolerances and processes—he's proceeding to the more creative level-two type of buying activity. Other chapters of this book will touch upon this value-oriented aspect of buying in more detail. But it's important to remember that being a good buyer starts with placing purchase orders—and purchase orders start with requisitions.

3

BETTER BIDS MAKE BETTER BUYS

Good purchases start with good requests for quotation—which are therefore an important part of the basic procurement cycle.

Anyone can call up a supplier and say, "Hey, Charlie—give me a price on 50,000 assorted grinch-plates!" (This is what makes back-door buying so popular. It's easy.)

A smart buyer, on the other hand, recognizes that soliciting bids is a vital part of his job and the entire purchasing process. It's not a job for amateurs. It's precisely when the requests for quote are about to go out that a buyer can make a hefty contribution of market know-how, business acumen, and other commercial skills.

The reason is that there are two important elements to handling quote requests: the "how" and the "who." The "how" concerns the methods for soliciting bids, and the "who" concerns the selection of the bidders' list. Both are important, and both are tasks for purchasing professionals.

As far as the "how" is concerned, you've got to remember that a request for quote is a highly specialized form of communication. Its purpose is three-fold:

1. To spell out just what the buyer wants, so that each bidder can quote intelligently;

2. To give the buyer all the facts he needs, after analyzing the returned quotes, to place the order;

3. To document the soliciting of bids and the reason for making the award.

There are, of course, many ways to request quotations. On relatively simple purchases, below whatever dollar figure the buying company wants to establish, the buyer may want to phone his inquiry to one or more potential suppliers. This technique is often used when the buyer's prime interest is availability of a stock item from a local source. Often, if he is told that the item is available for immediate delivery, he'll use the same phone call to give the vendor the go-ahead to ship.

Or, if he wants to check prices by phone with several local sources, he can note their verbal quotes right on the requisition for record purposes.

On other requirements, where the buyer wants a more formal record of quotations, he has several options open to him.

For complex proposals involving a lot of explanations, he may want to write a detailed letter to each bidder. This could be either a personal letter, or a form letter on a letterhead that's been imprinted for vendors' fill-ins.

In most cases, however, the buyer will probably want to use a request for quotation form. Even the smallest firms can buy stock request-for-quote forms from local stationers, and have them "personalized" by crash-imprinting of the buying company's name and address. One big advantage of such forms is that they usually are constructed with striped or patterned carbons. This allows several bidders' names to be typed during one insertion of the set into the typewriter—and it keeps each bidder from knowing who his competitors on the job are.

Other companies have custom-designed request for quote forms that are used across-the-board by all buyers. Fig. 3, for example, illustrates the request for quotation form used by Xerox Data Systems. This is a seven-part snapout form, which provides two copies each for three bidders, plus a work copy (illustrated) on which all bidders' names appear. (On the interior parts of the set, each bidder sees only his own name.) The form's heading also includes telephone area code and local phone numbers—always a sound bit of forms design on any external purchasing form.

But, no matter what the mechanics are for requesting quotes, there are specific facts that the buyer must keep in mind on any request.

For example, there is certain data that *must* be included on any quote request: quantity, description, and date the material is required. Without this information—presented clearly and unambiguously—the bidders simply cannot answer the inquiry.

In addition, there is certain data that the buyer *may* want to include on the quote request:

1. He may want to note any special terms and conditions that will apply to the order, from a legal point of view. (If a company's p.o. form includes detailed legal "boilerplate" on the back, the request for quote form should, too. This will eliminate subsequent delays caused by the supplier's objection to the legal terms.)

2. The buyer may also want to specify a firm closing date for receipt of all bids.

3. He may want to have each bidder specify how long his quote is good for.

4. If applicable, a request for return of blueprints may be in order.

5. A statement that all blueprints and drawings are confidential, and must be treated as such, is often desirable.

6. On complex jobs, that will require a lot of estimating time by bidders, the buyer may want to indicate whether the requirement is a firm one or is just for ballpark forecasting.

7. The buyer may want to ask for alternate proposals that will reduce costs or improve quality. Such requests can be either general in nature, or aimed at a particular area of the specifications (material, manufacturing process, etc.).

8. It may be necessary to specify who is to supply the material for the job, or the tooling.

9. If there are special quality tests that will apply, the buyer may want to note them.

10. The same holds true for special considerations regarding quantity. These might include allowable over-runs and under-runs; a request for price-break data; etc.

11. Finally, the buyer may want to specify how the bidder is to quote: by letter, on his own form, or on a copy of the buyer's form.

For buyers who specialize in a particular class of commodities, there may be items on the list above that apply to almost all their quote requests. If so, they should try to get the boss's approval to have a batch of the company's standard forms imprinted with the clauses or headings that apply. This will save a lot of time in the typing section—and will

XDS
Xerox Data Systems
555 South Aviation Blvd., El Segundo, California 90245
(213) 772-4511, 679-4511

THIS IS NOT AN ORDER

QUOTES MUST BE RECEIVED BY	RETURN TO:
	☐ ABOVE ADDRESS
FAILURE TO DO SO MAY RESULT IN ADDRESSEE'S NAME BEING REMOVED FROM BIDDER'S LIST	☐ P.O. BOX 913
MATERIAL FURNISHED BY	ATTENTION OF
☐ VENDOR ☐ XDS ☐ VENDOR EXCEPT AS NOTED	
COST OF TOOLING	F.O.B.
☐ AMORTIZED ☐ FURN. BY XDS ☐ PRICED SEPARATELY	
TERMS	SHIP VIA
VENDOR TO QUOTE PRICE EXACTLY PER PRINT OR SPECIFICATIONS	VENDOR TO SUBMIT ALTERNATE QUOTE WITH SUGGESTED DEVIATION FROM COLUMN 1.
COLUMN 1 ☐	SEE COL. II ☐

| ITEM | QUANTITY | DESCRIPTION | COLUMN | | DELIVERY SCHEDULE | |
| | | | 1 UNIT PRICE | 2 VARIANCE | XDS REQUEST | VENDOR PROMISE |

| COMPANY NAME | DATE | QUOTE AUTHORIZED BY | BUYER |

130 (10/69) XEROX DATA SYSTEMS ℗L

WORK COPY

Fig. 3 Request for quotation used by Xerox Data Systems is a seven-part snapout that provides two copies for each of three bidders, plus a work copy for buyer. Double-headed columns give space for bidders to suggest alternate proposals, if requested.

Denver, Colo._____ 19____

We have indicated by (x) below, the present status of your quotation
No._____, dated_____, which was submitted in reply to
our inquiry No._____, dated_____.

	WE HAVE PLACED ORDER AGAINST A MORE FAVORABLE OFFER.
	YOUR QUOTATION WAS RECEIVED TOO LATE TO BE CONSIDERED.
	YOUR QUOTATION IS STILL UNDER CONSIDERATION.
	WILL NOT BE PURCHASED. PLEASE CLOSE YOUR FILE.

STEARNS-ROGER CORP.
PURCHASING DEPARTMENT

FORM K-330 1M 2-69 ℗   **BY:**_____

REJECTED QUOTATION

Reference: Quote Req. _____
Your _____
of _____

Covering: _____
_____
_____
_____

We found it necessary to place our order for this material elsewhere due to following:

	Price too high.
	Delivery not acceptable.
	Quote rec'd too late.
	Substitute not acceptable.

Other: _____
_____
_____

CHAMPION
AMSCO   DISH WASHING MACHINE COMPANY
WINSTON-SALEM · NORTH CAROLINA · U.S.A.
Subsidiary of American Sterilizer Company

Date: _____   By: _____

Fig. 4 Quote acknowledgments—used by Stearns-Roger Corp. and Champion Dish Washing Machine Co.—promote good vendor relations for the price of a postcard.

16

make it easier for the buyer to analyze incoming bids.

In general, when bids come in, every buyer must check to see that each one is complete. At the very least, each quote must state price, availability, cash terms and f.o.b. point. And on some government jobs, bidders must also state their small or large business status and labor area classification.

Over and above this basic data, however, the buyer should examine each quote for the merit of alternate proposals, price break data, weight and routing information and special considerations such as packaging, cost information on returnable containers, etc. In some cases involving major raw materials, he may want to know the bidder's production capacity per day or week.

Unless the product or service that each bidder is offering is identical, the buyer has no real touchstone for comparing costs. As a result—and this is a matter of good business as well as of ethics—the buyer should usually let all bidders re-bid if he lets one re-bid.

Sometimes this practice may result in a design piracy charge from one bidder, and—in cases where one supplier has contributed a truly new concept—the buyer may decide to place the first order without further competition.

In general, however, the buyer should avoid any possibility of being tagged as one who plays favorites among suppliers. The only other exception to the "one re-bids, all re-bid" rule, therefore, should be when one bidder submits a quote that's ridiculously high or low. In such cases, the buyer may want to let that supplier re-bid—but he should do so without revealing whether the original quote was high or low.

Finally, after he has made his buying decision based on all quotes, the buyer can foster good vendor relations by notifying unsuccessful bidders.

This won't be necessary on every job, perhaps, but it's only common courtesy on major jobs, to let each bidder know how his proposal has fared.

Fig. 4, for example, illustrates two postcard forms, used by Stearns-Roger Corp. and by Champion Dish Washing Machine Co. They're excellent models of the simple techniques that can be used to promote solid vendor relationships during the buying process.

4

HISTORY CARDS TELL THE STORY

An important part of the basic purchasing cycle is the development of information on past and current buys. And, while some companies may have computers that store this data on tape or disc files, many other firms must rely on manual systems set up by the buyer.

That's why, in such companies, a purchase history card is a must. It will supplement the information on inventory control forms, to tell the buyer everything he needs to know about the items he's responsible for.

There may be cases where traveling requisition forms (discussed in the next section of this book) can take the place of history cards. But such double-use of the TR's depends on your purchasing set-up consistently meeting the following conditions:

1. Your purchases are all repetitive;
2. Every item is covered by a traveling requisition;
3. You rarely add items to stock;
4. Purchasing and production control, or other groups responsible for maintaining TR's, share office space;

18

5. You discuss purchased items with salesmen only at reorder time.

Since few if any purchasing departments will find themselves in this position, let's look at the basic purpose of the purchase history card and at the type of information it should carry.

There are two basic reasons for keeping history cards on the items you buy.

First, on repetitive items, the card provides an interim record that you can readily refer to when you don't have access to the traveling requisition on the item.

Second, on non-repetitive items, the purchase history card is your only means of recording such one-shot purchases.

In practical terms, this means that you can use the card for all sorts of notes and comments on repetitive items. You can record up-to-date bids, post new lead times, or jot down the names of possible new sources. The card is also useful for noting potential ordering combinations, such as "Check part No. 12345 for possible pooled run."

(As noted in Chapter 1, you should also see to it that at least some of this information is also on the inventory control group's stock record cards. But if you have it at your own desk too, you're in a much better position to take action on it.)

Then, when it's actually time to reorder the part in question, a quick review of the history card will automatically call all these matters to your attention. You won't have to keep all the data in your head. The chance of error will be appreciably lessened.

In addition, purchase history cards make it easy to set up systems where your secretary or a clerk assumes part of the clerical burden. Under such systems, the secretary or clerk simply pulls the appropriate history cards as soon as requisitions arrive in purchasing. Then she can turn all the documents over to you for review and action.

For training new buyers, too, purchase history cards are useful. They permit the new man to study ordering patterns in advance—at a time when there's no particular urgency. The alternative—waiting until requisitions arrive—sometimes means that there's no time for thoughtful study of the part's history. The current order may have to be placed too quickly.

On one-shot purchases, the prime advantage of purchase history cards is that they provide a formal record of such buys. This makes it easy for you to determine how often a supposedly non-repetitive item is cropping up for reorder. Then, if the frequency warrants it, you can arrange to make the part a stock item—and can set up a traveling requisition covering its regular procurement.

With the dual purpose of purchase history cards in mind, let's consider how these basic reference forms should be designed.

As far as size goes, you can pick whatever dimensions are handiest for you to work with. Many companies use fairly large sheets—8½ x 11 or even 8½ x 14. Their advantage is that more data can be packed onto one sheet, and the form will usually cover more transactions.

Many other firms, on the other hand, prefer to use smaller forms such as standard 5 x 8 cards. This enables them to use portable filing boxes, which the buyer can easily carry to his desk for ready reference. And many companies use special filing equipment—from trays to ring-books—which feature visible-edge displays of the shingled forms inside them.

But whatever size you choose for a purchase history card, the form itself should prominently feature the part number or item name. You will be filing the forms by number or name, so you'll want to do everything you can to make look-ups easy.

The history card should also include a brief description or an outline of the item's specifications. This doesn't mean that you have to include the complete text of highly technical specs on a part. Presumably, the complete specs are filed in engineering, manufacturing or some other department. All you have to do is note their existence and number—along with the dates of any engineering change notices—somewhere on the history card.

However, the purchase history card should contain enough technical data so that you can discuss the item intelligently with salesmen in between reorders. For example, the card should not only list size and nature of the item. It should also note basic raw material, unit weight, special packaging requirements, or any other factors that you feel are important.

The main body of the purchase history card should be devoted to a summary of all ordering activity. The best way to handle this is to list suppliers' names in a section coded 1-2-3 or A-B-C. In the sections devoted to recording actual purchases, you can then note the supplier's name by posting a single digit.

In the recap of orders, you'll undoubtedly want to include date, requisition or authorization number, p.o. number, vendor's coded identification, quantity and price.

You may also want to include trade discounts and (unless these are noted in the "supplier" section) cash terms and f.o.b. points.

Many firms also find it helpful to include delivery dates and quantities received. This means they have to set up a system for posting this data when the goods and receiving reports come in (which involves double look-ups and refiling). However, firms using this technique feel that the advantages outweigh the trouble and inconvenience. They get a

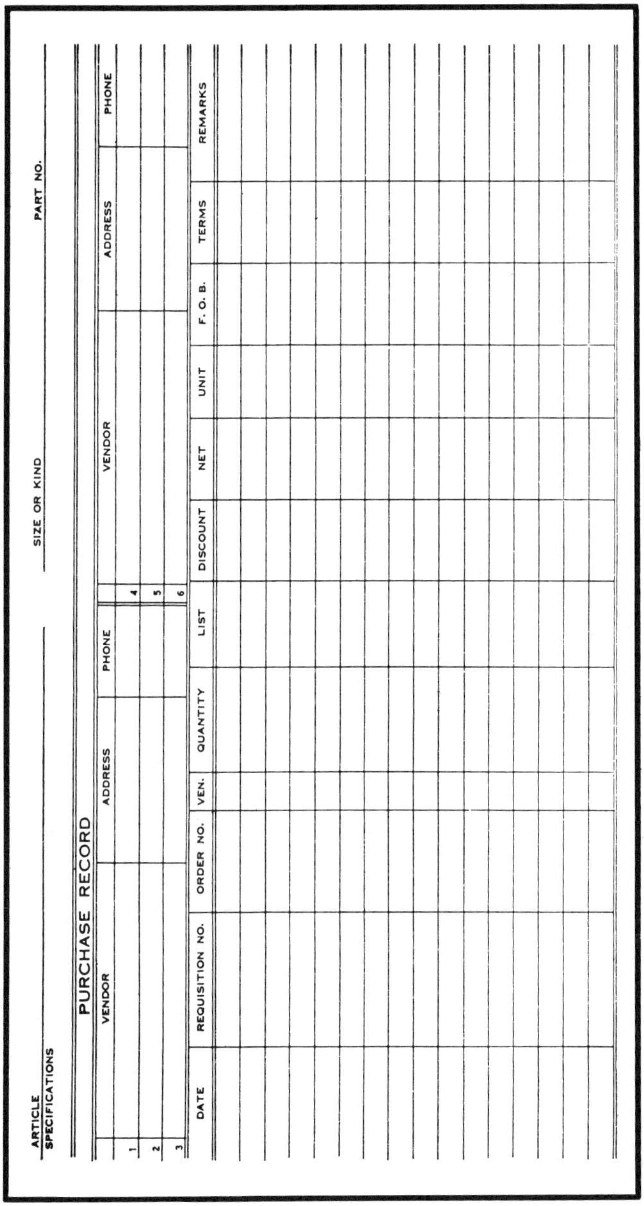

ARTICLE
SPECIFICATIONS
SIZE OR KIND
PART NO.

PURCHASE RECORD

	VENDOR	ADDRESS	PHONE		VENDOR	ADDRESS	PHONE
1				4			
2				5			
3				6			

DATE	REQUISITION NO.	ORDER NO.	VEN.	QUANTITY	LIST	DISCOUNT	NET	UNIT	F. O. B.	TERMS	REMARKS

Fig. 5 Purchase history card should give the buyer fast answers to any questions he may have. Face of form shown here lists part number and brief specifications, gives running record of purchases. Reverse side has spaces for recording between-reorder quotes.

reading on vendor performance in two areas: delivery, and over/under-runs.

Another section you may want to include on purchase history cards is one for recording new bids from both current and potential suppliers. If the data in this section is accurate and clearly spelled out, it may save you from having to send out quote-requests at reorder time.

The bid section of the history card should provide spaces for the dates of all quotes and, if possible, for the length of time that each quotation may be considered as in effect. It should also make it possible to list quotes for various quantities. For new bidders, there should be room for listing cash terms, lead times, f.o.b. points, etc. Without such additional data, each bidder's raw prices would be meaningless.

The final section of a well-designed purchase history card will be headed simply "Remarks."

In this section you can jot down notes and memos to yourself: anything from "Last order barely met specs," to "Call Harry in engineering before placing order."

Used in this way, a purchase history card becomes almost a diary of potential problems or other important matters. If you keep it up to date, you'll know it's complete and accurate when you refer to it. Or, if you're out of the office when an item comes up for reorder, somebody else in the department can get all the facts he needs from the card.

Because purchase history cards are used so often, and contain so much pertinent information, they sometimes become dog-eared and battered. More importantly, they sometimes become almost illegible. But if you want to make them useful and productive tools in your daily buying activities, you'll strive to see that this doesn't happen to the cards in your file. One way to do this is to make your notations as neatly as possible. And you can even make some entries in pencil, which can later be erased to leave room for more current entries.

Fig. 5 illustrates one purchase history card that's in actual use. For truly efficient buying, your daily activities should be built around some record similar to it.

5

VENDOR RECORDS KEEP FACTS ON FILE

To do a good buying job, you have to know your suppliers and your potential suppliers. You have to know their abilities and their attitudes—so gathering information on vendors is one of your biggest jobs.

Getting the data together, however, is only the first part of the task. You must also have some system for filing the information, and for retrieving it quickly when it's needed.

Ideally, the system should be one that doesn't entail too much paperwork at either end—input or retrieval. And one of the best ways to accomplish this is to recognize the various *types* of vendor information that must be kept available.

In general, vendor data that's worth saving falls into one of the following categories:

1. Product information regarding the goods or services that the supplier provides;

2. Background data concerning his technical ability and financial standing;

3. Hard facts about his actual performance on the job;

4. Topical information that you may need on a day-to-day basis. (Example: information on when the salesman last called. This might indicate when to expect him again.)

It's important to recognize these four information areas. Otherwise, you won't have any real basis for segregating the various bits and pieces of data that you accumulate on each vendor. Here's a rundown on each one:

Product information: In this area, your best bet is to build up a well-organized catalog file (see Chapter 8). Such a library will give you a big assist in your buying duties. It will also be a reference source for other company departments—automatically promoting better relations with engineering, manufacturing and other technical groups.

Background information: This type of data supplements your knowledge of various suppliers' product lines, by pinpointing how well equipped each one is to make and distribute his goods. You should therefore seek to accumulate as much pertinent data as possible in this area.

There are many ways to do this. One way is through personal visits to vendors' plants and warehouses. Another is to give vendors questionnaires to fill out and return. Still another is to jot down relevant facts during office interviews. But, no matter what technique or combination of techniques you use, there are many points that you should make a matter of record.

Typically, these would include a brief history of the supplier firm, a description of its plant layout, a list of equipment, names and backgrounds of key personnel, financial status (from the annual report or Dun & Bradstreet), common carriers serving the geographic area, union affiliations and contract expiration dates, and (if applicable) vacation shutdown schedules.

A brief rundown on other customers of the firm might also be a part of this background file.

Much information of this nature can be summarized on a form—and many buyers do use vendor data sheets or cards for recapping such factual material (see Fig. 6). Then, the data sheet can be brought up to date annually on major suppliers, and as often as desired on other vendors.

An alternative is to set up a letter- or legal-size folder on each vendor warranting a background file. Then you can add new material (current annual reports, announcements of staff additions or equipment

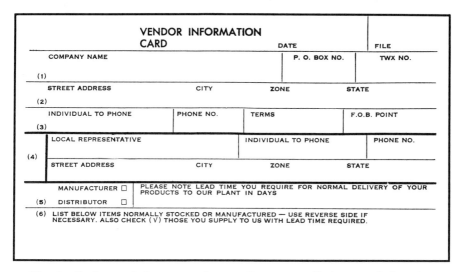

Fig. 6 Background data on major suppliers can easily be recorded on information cards like this one, or on 8½ x 11 sheets that provide even more space for pertinent entries. An alternative plan is to set up a background folder on each source, into which the buyer can drop material such as annual reports, equipment lists, etc.

changes) to the folder as necessary. At the same time, you can remove outdated material of this nature.

The background file thus serves as a handy repository for material that may be needed once in a while—but probably not too often. It should therefore not include detailed product references—which more properly belong in the catalog file—but should cover product capabilities resulting from the possession of particular equipment.

The broader you make the background file on any vendor, the more benefit it will be to you. For example, it may not really be pertinent whether the president of a vendor firm went to Harvard or Yale. But if a data sheet or record file indicates that the sales manager went to M.I.T., this at least indicates that you can look for some degree of technical competence from him. You may want to key the tone of negotiating sessions or other interviews accordingly.

Performance information: Whether or not you maintain a formal rating system on vendors' performance, there is specific data that you should have on tap regarding each major source.

The file for this data should include current information such as total dollar volume awarded each supplier (updated at least annually), and some sort of reading on quality, delivery, and service. The figures on dollar volume are important because they tell you your "net worth" to the supplier. You can use this figure in appraising how well the supplier *should* be servicing your account in all three areas: on-time shipments, product reliability, and technical service leading to cost reductions and other efficiencies.

One way to implement such a file is to set up another set of folders —one for each major supplier—into which you can drop copies of pertinent letters, memos, or forms.

Suppose that you have to write a hot letter to the president of the ABC Co., outlining delivery problems that you've been having with his firm. If you drop a copy of the letter into ABC's "performance" file, you'll have a ready-made record of the matter the next time the question of ABC's delivery performance arises.

Or, if you write a letter praising ABC for a workable cost reduction suggestion, a copy of that letter should also go into the file.

If you prefer, you can record suppliers' delivery performance by saving actual p.o. copies on orders that have suffered acute delivery problems. The expediter's annotated copies would be ideal for this purpose—especially if you wanted to whip them out of the file and wave them under the salesman's nose. Used in this way, each notation on the copies might well be an indication of a promise made but not kept.

Much the same technique can also be used to record quality deficiencies. In this case, you'll want to save an extra copy of each rejection report from incoming inspection. Whether you want to use such records in bargaining sessions on future orders or not, they'll still be useful to you. A quick riffle through them will give you a good picture of the supplier's quality/delivery performance.

Important: this information would also be available to a new buyer inheriting your commodities, or to another staffer filling in for you while you were on vacation or a business trip.

Topical information: The final type of information that you need centers largely around the salesman who represents the supplier: his name, his company (or companies, if he's a manufacturer's representative), how often he calls, the names of his inside sales service personnel, etc.

Much of this data may have to be listed on suppliers' background files, too. But for ready and easy reference, it's also possible to convert salesmen's calling cards into basic fact sheets.

At least one purchasing executive for a major manufacturing firm has developed this gambit into a highly workable procedure. As of two or three years ago, he had accumulated something like 750 business cards from supplier salesmen—keeping them in three trays designed especially for calling cards.

Whenever a salesman calls for the first time, this purchasing man accepts his card and looks it over. Many cards, of course, are already imprinted with data such as product lines. On those that don't carry such information, the purchasing agent pencils it in. Then he dates the card and files it.

On subsequent visits, he dates the card each time the salesman calls. For, as he puts it, "we feel that the salesman who will come in to see us at regular intervals . . . is more apt to give us better service than the man we rarely see."

If you'd like to adapt this method to your own purposes, there are several types of file units made just for calling cards. They range from acetate jackets that will hold several cards per jacket, and can be filed in ring binders, to devices that slot and spindle business cards for rotary wheel files.

Such units will at least spare you having a desk drawer with business cards scattered throughout it—or a completely unalphabetized (useless) packet of cards held together by a rubber band. And, if you play your cards right, they really can be part of the vendor records that keep facts on file for you.

6

THE PURCHASE ORDER:
BASIC BUYING DOCUMENT

The preparation of a purchase order is the moment of truth in buying.

This is when it all comes together: the need has been recognized; the authority to buy has come to the buyer in the form of a requisition; and the buyer has looked over his history records to get the background. He may also have checked his vendor data files to determine potential bidders, and may have solicited quotations based on which he has chosen one particular supplier.

In addition, he may have negotiated any number of matters with one or more vendors.

Since negotiation is such an important part of professional buying, it will be discussed separately in the following chapter. There are, however, three elements of any purchase order with which a buyer must be concerned. Here's a quick rundown on each of them:

Legal aspects: The first thing to remember is that a purchase order is basically a legal contract. It represents a meeting of the minds between the buying company and the supplier. And, if a purchase order ever gets to litigation in the courts, the p.o. form itself will be prime evidence to the court hearing the case.

This doesn't mean that oral contracts cannot also be binding on both parties. They can—and often, as will be seen, with far-reaching results. In actual practice, however, almost all of any buyer's contracts will be written on his company's purchase order.

Also, in most cases, the buyer will want to write a purchase order that is a firm contract rather than an open-ended price agreement or "hunting license." Probably the only instances where he doesn't want to commit himself are blanket orders and other long-term arrangements where he can't predict demand with 100% accuracy.

This means that the buyer must look at every purchase order to make sure that it not only represents a meeting of the minds—but that it calls for the "mutual consideration" that every legal contract requires. Each party to the order must guarantee to do something: the seller to make and/or deliver the goods, the buyer to accept them and pay for them if they pass inspection.

The second point a buyer must keep in mind is that, from a legal point of view, he represents the buying company. He is an "agent" of the company, just as the top purchasing man is (whether his title is "purchasing agent," "purchasing manager," or "vice president of purchases").

The law on agent/principal relations, moreover, is very clear. It states that third parties (such as suppliers) cannot be expected to know of special considerations or limitations applying to agent/principal relationships. This simply means that a buyer—even if his company has limited his p.o. approval authority—can legally commit his company to an outside source for dollars far in excess of his in-house limits.

The third legal point to keep in mind is that just about all purchases are today governed by the Uniform Commercial Code. The only state that hasn't adopted the UCC (which is based on English common law) is Louisiana (where the Napoleonic Code rather than common law is the foundation for current legislation).

The big difference between the Uniform Commercial Code and the Uniform Sales Act that it has replaced (and which wasn't very uniform, anyway) is one of philosophy. The UCC is business-oriented. It holds that if two parties want to have a contract, and act as though they have a contract—then they *have* a contract.

For buyers and sellers, one of the main effects of the Code is to change the ground rules of what happens when the buyer's purchase order and the seller's acknowledgment form carry differing terms and conditions.

Under the Uniform Sales Act, the terms on the buyer's purchase order constituted an "offer," and the terms on the seller's acknowledgment form constituted a "counteroffer." There was no contract until the seller shipped the goods and the buyer accepted them—usually under the terms and conditions of the last form sent between the two parties.

Under the UCC, both buyer and seller are held as having a contract despite differing terms on their forms. The terms where they're in agreement apply to that contract; the general provisions of the UCC apply to those where they're in disagreement.

For maximum protection, however, the buyer's purchase order form should carry a statement that only his terms and conditions shall apply; that any different terms proposed by the seller are objected to and rejected.

The seller, of course, can put a similar clause on his acknowledgment form. If he does, the two clauses wash each other out and both parties are on the same footing. If he doesn't, the buyer's terms will apply. (By the same token, if the seller's form carries such a blanket proviso and the buyer's doesn't, the seller's terms will apply.)

On oral or telephoned orders, the buyer has a "reasonable" time in which to send a written confirmation with whatever terms he wants. Then the seller has 10 days in which to reply with differing terms. In turn, the buyer then has 10 days to object to the seller's terms. Or, if the buyer doesn't send a p.o. confirmation at all, and the seller sends in a written set of terms on his own form, the seller's terms will apply.

Administrative aspects: The buyer's prime responsibility from an administrative point of view, in writing purchase orders, is to see that all his purchases meet the procedural requirements that his company has set up. If there is a procedures manual, or a set of general memos governing buying methods, it's the buyer's duty to follow the prescribed routines.

In any event, the buyer must set up a series of guidelines for his daily buying activities, to guarantee that at least each major purchase can subsequently be audited. Whether the auditing is done by an internal staff, or an outside group, purchasing records should indicate basic facts on each such buy.

These facts should include: authorization for the purchase (requisition), reason for selecting a chosen supplier (quote requests and bid analysis sheets), substance of the order (purchase order form), receipt of the goods (receiving report), acceptable quality (inspection report). This is the kind of information any auditing crew looks for in determining whether or not sound purchasing practices have been followed to justify payment of the invoice.

Of the facts listed above, the one that's most difficult to pin down is the buyer's reason for selecting the chosen supplier. The other facts can be documented by keeping good records, cross-indexed so an auditor can readily refer to them. But selection of suppliers is a more subjective matter—one that often involves a host of factors other than quoted prices.

The buyer's best bet, therefore, is to develop a set of guidelines or even a checklist with which he can justify his reasons for awarding various purchase orders.

Some companies have "basis of award" sheets like the one illustrated in Fig. 7. This makes it easy for the buyer to check off his reason or reasons, and make the sheet part of the basic records on each order. In other companies, the requisition form or request for quote master copy may have a similar list that can be checked off.

If a buyer is currently working under a set-up where such guidelines haven't been developed, he should take steps to have a set developed. One approach would be to ask for such guidelines from his immediate supervisor. Another would be to work up a set himself, and then present them to the supervisor for approval or possible modification.

Choosing suppliers, after all, is what the buyer is paid for. It's unrealistic to expect him to do it without ground rules.

Creative aspects: When a buyer signs any purchase order, or bucks it up the line for whatever purchasing approval is required, he should be sure in his own mind that the order represents the best possible purchase his company can make at that time. This is where the "level two" type of judgment mentioned in Chapter 2 is required: judgment that's based on technical knowledge of the commodities involved, commercial savvy of the marketplace, and large doses of imagination and salesmanship.

In practical terms, this means that the buyer should look at every requirement that hits his desk, to determine if it should be filled exactly "as-is," or could possibly be modified to improve ultimate value to the company. Since the buyer's desk is the last stop for all purchased requirements before they're fed into suppliers' order-processing routines, it's the spot where value analysis activity naturally centers.

Or, if a buyer contributes his ideas early in the design stage, before specifications are frozen, he's making himself an active participant in the "value engineering" studies that often provide a maximum payoff.

In either case, to prove that he's more than just an order-placer, the buyer has to be willing to question (if not challenge) the require-

PURCHASING DEPARTMENT

B A S I S   O F   A W A R D

P.O. # _____

Date _____

1.		This order placed on basis of previous competitive bidding on purchase order number.	
2.		Contact only one source: Item is standard price and non-competitive.	
3.		Most prompt delivery.	
4.		Better delivery anticipated on basis of past performance.	
5.		Difference in delivery outweighs price consideration.	
6.		Facilities on vendor chosen indicated greater ability to perform contract.	
7.		Shop practice and/or engineering has determined that the product chosen is preferable for economy, quality and operation.	
8.		Mandatory source required by engineering and/or customer.	
9.		All conditions equal: No preference.	
10.		Order was placed with vendor offering best available price, taking all factors into consideration.	
11.		No substitution allowed (patented material)	
12.		Cash discount considered.	
13.		Only known source.	
14.		Vendor has tooling in his possession peculiar to manufacture of this part.	

	VENDOR	Item 1	Item 2	Item 3	Item 4	Item 5	TOTALS
1.							
2.							
3.							
4.							
5.							

REMARKS: _____

_____

_____

_____

SIGNED _____   APPROVED _____

Fig. 7 Award justification sheets like this one pinpoint the buyer's reasons for supplier selection. Such a sheet, or a statement on the requisition or quote request form, should be part of the file on major purchases.

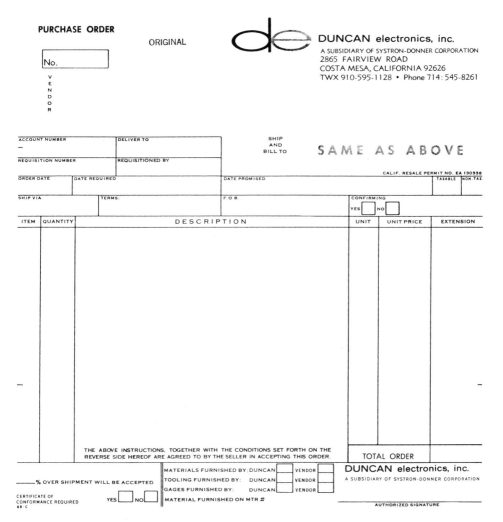

Fig. 8 Purchase order used by Duncan Electronics, Inc. is a snapout set with comprehensive terms and conditions on the reverse side. Different companies may use different styles of p.o., but the buyer's responsibility is always the same: to get the most value on every order he issues.

ments that are regularly presented to him. He has to scrutinize order quantities, specifications, tolerances, packing and shipping methods, and manufacturing processes. He has to be able to motivate suppliers to come up with new ideas, and his own technical people to run objective tests on such suggestions.

Here, for example, are just a few of the questions a value-minded buyer can ask himself no matter what type of items he's responsible for.

On raw materials: What is the material we're now buying? In what form do we buy it: strip, coil, bar, powder, liquid, etc.? Can we change the basic material without impairing function? How about finish? Or shape? Or the supplier's manufacturing method?

On fabricated parts: How are we now buying the part? Can we possibly change a forging to a casting, or a stamping to a wire-form? How about powder metal? Or cold heading? Can we reduce secondary machining? Are the tolerances specified necessary?

On capital equipment: Is the unit requested the best one for the job? Is there another model? Another brand? Special attachments that might boost efficiency? Have we checked out maintenance costs? Safety factors? Labor availability?

On supplies and services: Can we change material or size on supplies? Frequency of service on services? Can we pool orders for various departments? How about a standards program?

In framing such questions to himself, the buyer should keep one very important point in mind: value equals function divided by cost. The buyer can increase value in either one of two ways—by increasing function or reducing cost.

Like requisition forms—and, for that matter, like all basic forms in the procurement cycle—purchase orders come in many styles and designs. Fig. 8 illustrates an excellent one used by Duncan Electronics, Inc.

But, no matter what type of form a buying company uses, it's up to the buyer to get the most value from every purchase he makes.

7

NEGOTIATE FROM STRENGTH

Of all the mis-understood and mis-applied terms in the purchasing lexicon, "negotiation" probably heads the list. To many people—and this includes some in the purchasing profession as well as outsiders—the word has all sorts of tainted connotations. It conjures up images of Arabian street-bazaars, where buyers and sellers haggle and dicker over price.

In actual fact, however, nothing could be further from the truth. The whole process of coming to a meeting of the minds on any subject involves negotiation.

Suppose that you convince your wife (who has her heart set on a mink coat) that what she really wants for Christmas is a new vacuum cleaner. That's a successful negotiation. And so is the case where you sell your son on a deal where his continued participation on the school football team will depend on his maintaining a B average.

In your buying job, similarly, a successful negotiation is one where you and the supplier agree (come to a meeting of the minds) on the substance of the order in question. This means discussing each and every aspect of the order, which includes:

    (a) Quantity
    (b) Price
    (c) Delivery date
    (d) Specifications
    (e) F.o.b. point
    (f) Cash terms
    (g) Packaging
    (h) Legal terms
    (i) Inspection/certification techniques
    (j) Stocking arrangements

In many cases there may be other aspects of the order that you want to negotiate with the supplier. But even the list above is a fairly lengthy one—and the important thing is that each element on the list can often be broken down into sub-elements. This gives you a wide assortment of bits and pieces that you can use in arranging various tradeoffs during a negotiating session.

Under *quantity,* for example, you can discuss both original quantity requirements, and allowable overs and unders. You may be able to get a better price by boosting the original quantity to the supplier's next price break level. (You may even be able to negotiate that level downward.) Or, in discussing allowable overs and unders, you may decide that it's worth something to you in price if the vendor hits the order quantity exactly on the nose.

Specifications are an area where you may be able to do a great deal of negotiating—and this is true whether the specifications are expressed in absolute terms or as "performance" specs. In discussing mechanical, chemical or metallurgical specs, you can zero in on matters such as materials, manufacturing processes, tolerances and weights. And, on performance specs, you have similar latitude. You can negotiate not only such matters as how many pieces per hour or per day a supplier's equipment will turn out for you in your plant—you can also negotiate how many days it will take, after the original installation, to hit that production rate.

Or, on *stocking arrangements,* you will probably have to pose questions such as: "Will the supplier make and hold goods for you? How much or how many will he make and hold? How much extra, if anything, will he charge for providing this service? To what extent will his delivery performance improve under such a set-up? Will he guarantee (and this is what negotiation is all about) that improved delivery performance?"

As a practical matter, probably 75% or more of all the negotiations you ever participate in will center on delivery. Reason: it's something you have to consider on every order you place, even on standard shelf items. But there will be cases when you and the supplier have to literally pick the upcoming order apart, to analyze each of its elements. This is particularly true on custom-made fabricated parts or assemblies. Here's a brief rundown on some of the points to remember when you're negotiating such orders:

The first point to keep in mind is that every negotiating session forces you to handle two jobs concurrently if not simultaneously. You have to sell the supplier on what you want for your company; and you have to make him justify what he wants for his company.

The second point to remember is that good negotiating requires careful planning. You have to decide in advance, at least in general terms, what aspects of the order are most important from your firm's point of view. You have to assign priorities to each of these elements. You have to decide what each one is worth in relation to the others.

The third point is an extension of the second. You also have to make an estimate of what aspects of the order will be most important to the supplier. Wherever possible, you should try to identify any matters that are relatively unimportant to you, but will probably be important to him. (Possible example: the particular machine on which he will run your job.)

The fourth point concerns the make-up of the negotiating team that you have to put together for full-scale negotiating sessions. The technical staffers from your own company, whose assistance you may require in thrashing out specifications, should be fully qualified in whatever state-of-the-art is under discussion. They should also agree in advance that you as buyer will be the spokesman for the negotiating team.

The fifth point is a legal one. You have to make sure that the negotiators representing the supplier have the authority to commit their firm. If you're dealing with an officer of a vendor's firm, you'll have no problems in this area. But, when you're talking to salesmen or engineers, you have to get this point nailed down.

The sixth point concerns the actual conduct of the negotiations— and this is an area where a large dose of common sense will pay off just as much as some of the more cloak-and-dagger routines sometimes recommended.

These arcane rituals include: seating your adversaries on uncomfortable chairs; positioning them so the sun is in their eyes or they're in an air conditioner's draft; breaking them up into small groups around the negotiating table; setting up elaborate signalling systems for your own negotiating team.

These ploys, however, may boomerang. If you put your opponents in an uncomfortable position, you may very likely get their backs up so they'll be even more unyielding in their positions. If you split them up around the table, your own team will be split up, too—unless you have twice as many people to start with. And, while a few discreet hand signals to your team-mates may not be completely out of place, this is a technique that can easily be overdone. (You may wind up looking like a self-conscious baseball manager trying to notify batter and runner that the hit-and-run is on.)

There will be cases, of course, where you may want to modify your game-plans during the course of a negotiating session. Usually the best way to do this is simply to call a recess so you and your team-mates can privately review what's happened so far. If the supplier's team has dropped some particularly pertinent comment that re-shapes your thinking, simply stall things along for ten or fifteen minutes before you call the recess. In this way, you won't tip the other side off as to what particular point has triggered your "caucus."

To some extent, as the preceding paragraph implies, negotiation is a guessing game. You don't want the supplier to know how far you're willing to concede points, and he doesn't want you to know how far he will go. So, as you conduct your negotiations, you will undoubtedly want to use such common-sense techniques as falling silent occasionally, and constantly seeking to trade small concessions for big ones. (Some people, such as salesmen, simply cannot abide a protracted pause in a conversation, and will blurt out almost anything to fill the void. If you know the absolute goals and limits of what will be a successful contract from your company's point of view, you can chip away at the supplier's position by offering tradeoffs within those limits.)

Aside from guesswork, however, there are two negotiating tools based on fact that every buyer should be familiar with. They are the learning curve and cost/price analysis. Their skilful use can often be brought into play in making suppliers justify their negotiating demands.

The learning curve is simply a scientific expression of an age-old adage: "practice makes perfect." The more times anyone does anything, the more proficient he becomes at it—whether the job in question is building a boat or shoeing a horse.

In business negotiations, you can use the learning curve to make the supplier justify his labor costs on repeat jobs, or on long-run jobs where learning gained on the first stages will benefit him on the latter stages.

Depending on the items you buy, various degrees of learning curve may apply to the supplier's manufacturing techniques. In the aircraft industry, for example, an 80% learning curve is often used and accepted by both negotiating parties. This simply means that per-unit labor costs go down 20% every time the quantity produced is doubled. The average per-unit cost of the first two units will be 80% of that of the first unit alone; the average per-unit cost of the first 20 will be 80% of that of the first 10; the average per-unit cost of the first 100 will be 80% of that of the first 50; and so on.

This means that the big benefits of the learning curve come in the early stages, and then tail off toward the end.

If you chart an 80% learning curve on square-grid graph paper, it will result in a hyperbola as illustrated in the upper chart in Fig. 9. Or, if you plot it on log-log graph paper, it will come out as a straight line as illustrated in the lower chart. The latter type of presentation is often more useful when you want to project the effect of the learning curve on future requirements that have to be manufactured.

On many orders, you may not have to go to the extent of charting learning curve efficiencies. Or you may not even be able to get suppliers to concede a specific percentage for a learning curve applicable to their business. But one thing they do have to concede (or admit that their manufacturing people are all a bunch of ninnies) is that there is such a thing as the learning curve. Any new operation or process automatically becomes more efficient as the ones performing it become more familiar with it. And, as the debugging process continues, the supplier's increased efficiencies should be reflected in lower prices. So, whether you use it formally or informally, the learning curve provides you with valuable bargaining ammunition on many negotiations.

Cost/price analysis, in turn, is the study of all elements of a supplier's costs, to determine if his prices are fully justified by those costs.

Some suppliers may be reluctant to furnish you with this kind of data. Perhaps your own boss may not be too keen on the idea—feeling that how the vendor arrives at his selling prices is none of purchasing's business. If this is the case, you simply have to do a little selling job.

In dealing with sellers who want to keep their costs confidential, you can point out to them that this attitude automatically shuts the door on any ideas you or your technical people might come up with. These ideas could include new methods for ordering material, setting up tooling, producing parts, making assemblies, or packing and shipping the product. In many cases, the supplier might be able to adapt the ideas to similar items sold to other customers, and increase his sales across the board.

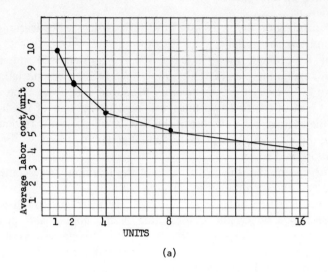

(a)

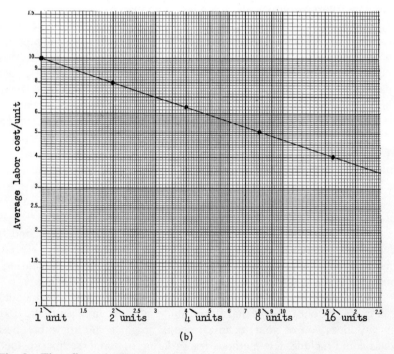

(b)

Fig. 9 The effect of a learning curve can be charted either on conventional graph paper (a.) or on log-log paper (b.). Both illustrations show decreasing labor costs caused by 80% learning curve: 1 unit @ $10, 2 units @ $8, 4 units @ $6.40, 8 units @ $5.12, 16 units @ $4.096.

In trying to sell your boss on using cost/price analysis, your most potent argument is that refusal to use the technique may keep you from getting the best price. It may also inhibit quality and delivery.

If all else fails, remind your boss that one of the most scurrilous comments sometimes directed at the purchasing profession is: "Any damn fool can look at three bids and decide which is the lowest." And point out to him that cost/price analysis is one of the techniques that make purchasing a truly creative and analytical function that goes far beyond "picking the lowest bid."

At the other extreme, your company may have a separate cost/price analysis group to support the purchasing staff. Even if it doesn't, you can still practice cost/price analysis on a do-it-yourself basis. The first thing that's necessary is an understanding of the various elements that make up a supplier's quoted price.

You can usually assume that this price represents the following: direct material costs, direct labor costs, factory costs, general and administrative costs, and profit.

The next step is to break each of these costs down into its separate elements, so that you can ask the supplier for data on each sub-element.

Direct material costs ordinarily consist of subcontracted items, raw materials, and purchased parts. You should therefore ask the supplier which components he contracts to other sources, and what he pays for them. You should also have him identify the types and prices of raw material he buys for your product, and the weight of each per part.

In addition, the supplier should give you a rundown on the major purchased items he buys for your product, and the price for each. If he has other substantial elements of direct material costs to contend with, he should identify them.

Computation of direct labor costs is primarily a matter of wage rates and hours. The best bet here is to ask the supplier to break out the various types of labor required to produce your part: set-up, fabrication, assembly, and any special operations. Then have him indicate how many hours of each type of labor are required for each step, and the applicable wage rate for each one. Multiplying hours times rates, adding up the answers, and applying a percentage for labor burden, then gives a total direct labor cost.

Much the same technique can be used in assessing engineering and other factory costs, if they are required on the job. Special costs for outside work such as heat treating or plating should also be included as part of factory costs.

The total of material, labor and factory costs will ordinarily be the figure to which the supplier applies a percentage for general and administrative overhead. Then he applies a percentage for profit to the result, to arrive at a selling price. He should indicate these figures to you as part of the cost analysis.

Once you have the information from the supplier, the next step is to determine if the data jibes with what you—and others in your company—know about the products and processes in question. You'll undoubtedly want to discuss the cost breakdown with people from manufacturing, engineering and other technical groups. You may also want to talk over the supplier's costing techniques with your own cost accounting department.

Based on your own industry and commodity knowledge, for example, you might be able to suggest revisions in the supplier's order quantities or sources. Such action might lower his costs in any one or all three of the cost elements pertaining to materials.

At the same time, your engineering and manufacturing people might be able to suggest alternate production processes: using multiple-station equipment in place of single-station units, working out numerically controlled tooling set-ups, etc.

In any case, even if they can't come up with specific new routines for making the product, your technical people can fill you in on whether or not the supplier's costs are in line. Analyzing such costs is an important part of their work on make-or-buy studies, estimating, etc. And then you can use this kind of information in factual, down-to-earth negotiation with the supplier.

As you get deeper into cost analysis work with your vendors, you will undoubtedly expand your own technical knowledge. You'll also find that many suppliers have cost/price analysis programs of their own—based on which they can give you data on their suppliers' and suppliers' suppliers' operations.

In journalism, there's an old adage: "Get behind the handout." It means that a reporter or editor shouldn't simply accept press releases without questioning them—for accuracy, significance, etc.

For buyers, a neat paraphrase might be: "Get behind the quotation." Cost/price analysis is the way to do that, and it will truly help you to negotiate from strength.

PART TWO

Back-up Aids and Simplified Systems

By its very nature, purchasing generates a great deal of paperwork—more, perhaps, than any other department in the company.

One reason is that the purchasing job involves the disbursal of large sums of money. The ways in which this money is disbursed, and the rationale for spending it with the sources that purchasing has chosen, must be fully documented as a matter of good accounting practice.

There's another reason that may not be quite so obvious. It's the fact that purchasing is not only a money-processing job, but an information-processing one as well. And information, in turn, is a combination of *data* and *ideas*.

The data may be facts and figures collected over a given period of time. The ideas may be opinions or forecasts, often supported by the historical data that has been gathered. But, whatever its composition, the information has to be processed before it can be put to practical use in a company's plans and strategies.

This means that there must be a master plan for collecting infor-

mation; for validating or authenticating the data; for weeding out unimportant details; and for transmitting the information to interested individuals in the most workable form. Unless a company has gone to a
highly computerized "management information system" ("M.I.S." in the
current jargon of the EDP trade), chances are this whole process of in-
formation-handling will involve a sea of paperwork.

Unfortunately, although this sea of paperwork may contain a wealth
of critical information—specifications, delivery requirements, stock levels, use patterns, etc.—it's also possible for the buyer to drown in it.
Or, if he doesn't actually go under, he may spend all his time treading
water just to keep afloat.

It's for this reason that the development of back-up aids and simplified systems—to streamline procedures without forfeiting accounting and
other controls—is a vital part of the purchasing job.

Depending on his company's organization, and the degree of auton-
omy he's given in developing such procedures, the buyer's role in systems improvements will vary. If his company has a methods or industrial engineering staff that he can call on for assistance, the buyer's main
responsibility may be outlining the particular problems he faces in recording information and channeling it to the proper parties. The systems
specialists can then make proposals and the buyer can review them in
terms of their practicality.

In smaller firms, subject to the top purchasing man's subsequent
approval, the buyer himself may get into systems analysis and studies.
If he does, he should keep in mind that the prime purpose of such studies
is to (a) eliminate paperwork wherever possible, through techniques such
as one-write procedures; (b) speed the movement of paperwork as much
as possible; (c) increase the accuracy of the paperwork to begin with.

In many cases, these goals have interlocking and cumulative effects.
Increasing the accuracy of paperwork, for example, often increases the
speed at which it moves, because it may eliminate verifying and re-check-
ing operations.

Most important of all, the development of back-up aids and simplified systems will give the buyer more time for doing a professional buying job, unburdened by clerical details.

8

HOW TO SET UP A CATALOG FILE

One of the most important back-up aids you can develop is a catalog file. Catalogs provide vital information for purchasing and other departments—but they have to be up-to-date, properly indexed and readily available. Since it's usually a buyer's job to maintain the catalog library, you should have an organized method for keeping a product and commodity data current and easy to refer to.

In big companies, there may be a full-time catalog library, or a clerk who handles product literature as part of central files. Such set-ups, however, don't void the buyer's responsibility. Although librarians or clerks can classify, index and arrange printed material for easy reference, the buyer must still screen what goes into the catalog file. He should also review what's in the file regularly, to determine what should be junked.

In smaller companies, the buyer should have some knowledge of how to code and record the receipt of product literature, and how to file it for maximum efficiency.

This means that buyers must be familiar with three main questions:

1. What should go into the catalog file;
2. How the file should be maintained;
3. The best methods for indexing the material.

The answer to the question of what should go into the catalog file is relatively easy. In general, the file should include any and all factual data pertaining to products and commodities. This would include buying guides such as the *Conover-Mast Purchasing Directory,* and literature furnished by suppliers: catalogs, technical data sheets, one-page bulletins, fliers, availability notices, etc.

Literature furnished by trade associations and other industry groups may also be included in the catalog file.

In gathering this material, however, you've got to be selective. You can't affort to retain every scrap of vendor-supplied literature on the off-chance that it may be needed some day. If you do, you'll quickly build an impressive-looking library—but chances are that much of the material will be of little value.

Your best bet is to ask yourself two questions as you scan each piece of incoming literature. The first question is: "Do we have, or will we have, any interest in this product area?" The second question is: "Will this literature be of any value if someone does refer to it?" (Purpose of the second question is to weed out promotional "puff pieces" that suppliers have purposely designed to look as though they contained hard information.)

To keep the catalog file active and current, you also have to know how old each piece of filed literature is, and how frequently it's referred to. One problem here is that appearances can be deceiving. An old catalog that's never been referred to will probably look "newer" than a more recent one that's already dog-eared from frequent use.

One way to keep track of catalog "aging" is to set up a master list of all printed pieces added to the file, with date of receipt and a brief identification. You can use this list in establishing cutoff points for regular reviews of the filed material. Anything over two or three years old, for example, should probably get a closer scrutiny for usefulness than more recent additions to the file.

Another good technique is to date stamp the cover or flyleaf of catalogs when they're first filed. This gives anyone using the file the ages of various catalogs at a glance, and serves as a cross-check on the master chronological file.

Some catalogs, naturally, are used every day. There's no real need to keep track of how frequently these are referred to. But for booklets that are needed only once in a while, it's a good idea to record use patterns.

One easy method to do this is to date and initial the catalog each time you pull it out for reference. These informal jottings can be placed on the flyleaf or on the margin of the first page. Then, unless there are special circumstances, you can be absolutely ruthless in throwing out booklets that have never been referred to during their tenure in the catalog file.

With these relatively simple techniques, you can keep your catalog file to manageable size. But at the same time you have to see to it that all potentially useful booklets are added to the file. To do this, you should let suppliers know the types of literature that you're looking for—and you should insist that visiting salesmen update their portions of the file regularly. (Don't worry about their seeing their competitors' catalogs farther down the shelves; that will just keep them on their toes.)

If you want to, you can also keep an informal "log" of how often and how well salesmen update and service your catalog files. As an indicator of supplier cooperation, you might make this information part of a vendor rating program.

The third area of cataloging that concerns the buyer is filing and indexing—and this whole problem would be much easier if suppliers would stick to standard formats for their literature. But, since they don't, most catalog files are necessarily a collection of hardbound books, pamphlets, ring binders and single sheets.

Ideally, despite variations in size and shape, all of this material should be filed as a common group. And for easy reference and access, the best type of equipment is open-front: shelving, book-cases, or open-shelf files.

Arranging fairly thick catalogs on open shelving is no problem because the bulk and rigidity of these volumes keep them upright even without dividers or spacers. Flimsier booklets, however, need special equipment to keep them neat and accessible.

One good system is to accumulate skinny pamphlets and one-page sheets in gusseted filing jackets or library boxes. These filing containers (available from most stationers) can then be arranged across one or more shelves of the catalog file. Labeled with their contents, they will keep the sheets inside them orderly and neat—and won't interfere with the placement of the heavier, more rigid books.

Also, since each of these containers holds only two inches or so of material, you can file and refile at random within each unit.

In general, however, organization of the entire catalog file must be based on a logical filing method.

PRODUCT		SUPPLIER		MFR.	DISTR.	REC'D.
Our No.	Their No.	No. PP.	Section		Row	Shelf

	LOANED TO		Date			LOANED TO		Date
Name	Dept.	Date	Ret.	Name		Dept.	Date	Ret.

Fig. 10 Catalog index card should indicate basic data about each publication in the file, and can also be used to record charge-outs.

Depending on circumstances, you may want to file literature alphabetically by vendor, alphabetically by product, or chronologically by date of receipt.

Filing alphabetically by vendor is probably the simplest method—and makes it easy for supplier reps to review and update their catalog file sections.

Filing alphabetically by product is a bit more sophisticated—and is a good system for a firm with a fast-expanding product line. It makes for easy reference when an engineer or designer comes in and says, "Where can we get such-and-such a component?"

Filing chronologically by date of receipt makes it easy to add material to the file, because this system is "open-ended." There is no need to leave gaps in the file for future additions.

However, since filing by date of receipt assigns arbitrary numbers to filed material, a cross-index is an absolute must with this system. The best approach is to set up standard index cards—one set listing suppliers alphabetically, and the other listing products alphabetically.

Under this set-up, you indicate on each card the chronological control number assigned to the filed literature in question. The same technique can also be used for cross-referencing material filed alphabetically by vendor or product.

As a general rule, all index cards should also include information on whether the catalog is a manufacturer's or distributor's edition, and should identify the catalog by supplier's form number or publication number. This number is usually printed on the front or back cover or title page, and will avoid ambiguity in any correspondence you may have with the supplier regarding the catalog.

As shown in Fig. 10, catalog index cards can also be designed to double as charge-out records in cases where you loan the books to other departments. You may also want to stamp all catalogs "Return to Purchasing Department," as a reminder to those who may have borrowed catalogs and are keeping them longer than need be.

In any case, a well-organized catalog index will help keep the file working at top efficiency both for purchasing and other groups that need product information.

Once you've set up an efficient catalog file you may find that more and more people are coming from other departments to use it. If so, you may want to establish an informal "information center" within purchasing, where plant personnel can check out product data. Simply place the catalog file somewhere near the entrance to purchasing; try to find an unused desk or table that can be positioned adjacent to the file; and add a supply of pencils and writing pads. With these few steps, your information center will be complete.

9

HOW TO PLAN AN INTERVIEW

Interviewing, in the broadest sense of the word, is a key part of every buyer's job.

No matter how technically competent a buyer may be, or how incisive his analytical skills, lack of interviewing ability invariably lessens a man's contribution to his company.

The reason is that any interview has one basic purpose: the passage of information. This is true whether the buyer is interviewing a salesman, a supplier's technical representative, or someone from his own company.

In any of these situations, the communication is face-to-face. The buyer has a unique opportunity to present information of his own, to observe his visitor's reactions, and to listen to what the visitor has to say on any particular subject.

In such a personal dialogue, the buyer may learn a great deal just from the other person's tone of voice, or from his facial expressions. This immediacy is lacking in other forms of communication such as letters, telegrams or phone calls. An interview therefore offers an unparalleled chance to exchange information without misunderstandings or ambiguities.

Since communication of information is a vital part of the buyer's duties, this means that he should cultivate his interviewing skill. While some people are by nature more articulate than others, there are certain interviewing techniques that can be learned through study and practice.

The first thing to remember is that good interviews don't just happen. They're the result of diligent homework, with plenty of planning.

Step one in preparing for an interview is to identify the main purpose of the meeting. Although the primary theme of any interview is "information," there are many variations on this theme. The buyer should first determine whether the reason for the meeting is to obtain general information, pass on general information, obtain specific information, or pass on specific information.

A typical purchasing interview may be geared to several or even all of these purposes. The buyer might want to learn the status of a particular order, and at the same time pass along the word that his company is coming out with a new product line.

In such circumstances, the purpose of the interview would be twofold: to obtain specific information (order status), and to provide general information (the new product line). And later interviews, quite likely, would be aimed at probing the supplier's ability to provide specific parts or components for the new product.

If an interview has more than one purpose, the buyer should allow time for all of them when he plans the schedule of the meeting. This is basically a matter of organizing his own thoughts in advance, so that the interview follows a logical pattern. Without such organization, the buyer and his visitor may wind up trying to talk about two different things at the same time.

Another advantage of mentally organizing each interview in advance is that this focuses attention on matters where the buyer can perhaps delegate part of the discussion to someone else in purchasing.

Many firms, for example, have a standing rule that salesmen calling on buyers must first stop by the appropriate expediter's desk and brief the expediter on the status of open orders before discussing other matters with the buyer. (This technique of opening all interviews with a discussion of open orders is one that any buyer can use, even when he does his own expediting.)

Once the buyer has determined the basic purposes of an interview, his next step should be to marshal the facts he'll need in conducting the meeting. He should systematically collect (a) the data he wants to present to the visitor, and (b) any background information that would be helpful in interpreting what the visitor may have to say.

Suppose that a buyer wants to discuss the possibility of a supplier's furnishing a new part. To prepare for the interview, the buyer would undoubtedly get together drawings, prints, specifications, and an estimate of first-run quantities. This would be the data for presentation *to* the supplier.

But, to help him analyze the statements he will probably get *from* the supplier ("Of course I can make that part, Charlie!"), the buyer should also collect other information. In the example we're talking about, he'd probably want to jot down an informal record of the supplier's actual performance in furnishing other similar parts in the past.

Such a record should include former order numbers, brief descriptions of the old parts, plus short comments on the supplier's success in meeting delivery promises, keeping quality levels, and offering cost reduction suggestions.

As another example, let's suppose a buyer has scheduled an interview with a supplier who consistently over-runs orders for custom made parts. In this case the buyer should not only assemble a record on quantities ordered and received from that supplier, he should also make a similar listing on orders awarded to the guilty supplier's competitors.

Armed with this data, the buyer will have a ready made answer when the supplier pleads (as he probably will) that "Everybody in the industry has to over-run."

In addition to determining the purpose of each meeting, and collecting information accordingly, another important part of interview planning is analysis of the other participants.

This doesn't mean that the buyer should try to be a swivel-chair psychologist. But it does mean that he should give some thought to the background, status, technical qualifications and general make-up of the people he'll be interviewing.

As noted in Chapter 6, for example, it's quite possible that a supplier salesman may not have the authority to commit his firm. If so, the buyer might waste a great deal of interview time simply by talking to the wrong person.

Similarly, in interviewing a technically trained salesman, the buyer can pitch his discussion to a more complex level than he can when dealing with an untrained sales rep. Moreover, foreknowledge of the salesman's basic personality can be a big help to the buyer in controlling the interview.

Usually the buyer will have no trouble in drawing a salesman out.

Most salesmen are highly skilled at verbalizing—but this isn't always synonymous with communicating.

The buyer should be able to predict just how expansive and discursive his visitor is likely to be. If he anticipates trouble in this regard, he can plan steps to keep the conversation keyed to the main issue, and to terminate it discreetly when all points have been covered.

For joint interviews such as full-scale negotiating sessions, there are other details that the buyer must take care of.

He must decide who is to attend, choose a meeting site, make sure that everyone will be available at the appointed time or have a back-up substitute ready, and notify each participant of files or records that should be brought to the session.

In addition, the buyer should check the physical facilities of the meeting place. He should make sure that the room is big enough to accommodate everyone; that there are enough chairs; that scratchpads and pencils are available; and (if necessary) that electric outlets are accessible for various types of product demonstrations.

At the end of any interview, there should be no doubt in anyone's mind as to just what was covered during the meeting. One way to accomplish this is to have each participant make a concise verbal summary just before the session closes.

Typically, such statements should include not only what has been covered, but should also pinpoint any matters not yet resolved and nailed down. It may also be desirable to reach an agreement on who is to be responsible for follow-up on such "open" items.

Also, before the interview breaks, the buyer should establish a tentative date and meeting place for the next session. It's usually easier to take care of this while matters are still fresh in everyone's mind, rather than waiting until later.

In any event, if the buyer makes a conscious effort to improve his interviews, his value to the company will rise proportionately.

10

TRAVELING REQUISITIONS:
FIRST STEP TO SYSTEMS

You're missing the boat as a buyer if you don't set up (or convince your boss to set up) traveling requisitions wherever possible in your purchasing operations.

One reason is that traveling requisitions (also known as "permanent" or "repeating" requisitions) save time for everyone involved in the procurement cycle.

They eliminate the need for requisitioners to rewrite the same data time after time.

They speed buyers' reviews of requisitions, since there's no need to edit item descriptions.

In addition, TR's make it easy for the order typist, who doesn't have to contend with handwritten scrawls as she transcribes constant data onto the purchase order form.

Finally, traveling requisitions can often be adapted to even more sophisticated systems applications. If they're properly designed to begin with, they will be a big help in making the move to automated order writing, or in turning small orders into big ones.

Suppose that you have discovered a group of commodities on which purchases are repetitive. The items might be anything from production goods to maintenance supplies. As long as you buy them over and over again, they are candidates for traveling requisition treatment.

Your first step, then, should be to recognize that there will be three individuals (or groups of individuals) using the TR forms. These persons are (a) the requisitioner, who will enter quantities needed and received, and dates; (b) the buyer, who will use the form in determining vendor, price and terms; and (c) purchasing's order typist, who will use the TR as a source document when she types the purchase order.

To make the form as easy to use as possible as it travels to various stations during the buying cycle, you'll want to consider factors such as the form's size, layout and construction.

As far as size is concerned, you can make a TR as small or as large as you want. Some firms get by with 3″ x 5″ index cards, while others use manila folders that can hold letter-size notes or memos inside them. But, whatever size you choose, make sure that each section of the form is big enough to accommodate all entries posted in normal handwriting.

In addition, there are six more points you may want to consider:

1. Use a good grade of card stock—at least 25% rag—heavy enough to withstand the rigors of repetitive use.

2. Check the possibility of printing the forms as visible-edge records, suitable for retention in special racks, trays or vertical files. Since the requisitioner may have hundreds of TR's in his file—each one paired with a matching inventory record—a fast scanning system will help him keep track of the items he controls.

3. Print the complete layout of the form, including constant data headings such as part number and description, on both sides. This means using a little bit more space. But it eliminates the need to flip the card over in referring to entries made on side two.

4. Color code the TR's assigned to various groups using them: stockroom, material control, etc. If each requisitioning department uses a different color TR card, it simplifies things in purchasing immensely. For one thing, it makes routing to the proper buyer almost automatic. And, when it's time to return the TR's to their respective groups, the color coding prevents mis-fires in the internal mail.

5. Make sure that the layout of the TR closely follows that of the purchase order form. This will make typing chores easier. The typist won't have to shift her eyes all over and around the TR as she types down the p.o. This is such an important point that it's worth joint redesign of both forms, if necessary.

6. Use ink other than black (sepia, perhaps) to lend emphasis to typed and handwritten entries. Or, as another way to help the typist hit top order-writing speeds, use tint-blocks to highlight the areas from which she takes data.

Design ideas such as these are aimed primarily at improving the traveling requisition's function in a manual, more-or-less conventional system. There are, however, many ways in which a TR procedure can be further refined.

One of the most common of these is to use the TR as a basic input for automated order-writing. With this method, constant data such as part number, name and specs is punched into a paper card or tape. The card or tape can then be inserted into the reader device of a semi-automatic typewriter—and the machine keys out the order at faster-than-human speeds. (With similar "header cards" for vendors' names and addresses, maintained in purchasing, the same high speeds can be realized on the name/address section of purchase orders. Then the only manual entries are quantity wanted, price, and date needed.)

For such automated order writing systems, the traveling requisition must be designed either as an edge-punched card (which can be fed directly into the special typewriter), or with some sort of pocket or envelope. The latter construction makes it possible to keep cards or paper tapes with the TR's to which they pertain.

In other systems, traveling requisitions can be used to coordinate purchases of similar items, to build up order-quantities. With this technique, each TR covers a broad family of like products, so that pooled-buying possibilities are immediately pinpointed. The method is particularly appropriate for maintenance supplies, which just about always come in a wide variety of sizes, types and finishes. One form, for example, might cover all washers, nuts, bolts—or office items such as paper stocks. Then, when both the inventory specialist and the buyer work with the form, they're automatically reminded of pooled-order possibilities.

Such a technique obviously makes it necessary to list a variety of specs on each TR—and this in turn cuts down on the number of buying transactions that can be recorded. But, in the long run, this is a small price to pay for the extra buying efficiency.

Still another systems gambit to which TR's can be adapted is to team the forms up with office copying equipment.

With confidential data such as vendors' names and prices masked out by overlays, the TR's can be run through copiers to produce tabulations of item activity. Or, with different overlays that let just one vendor's

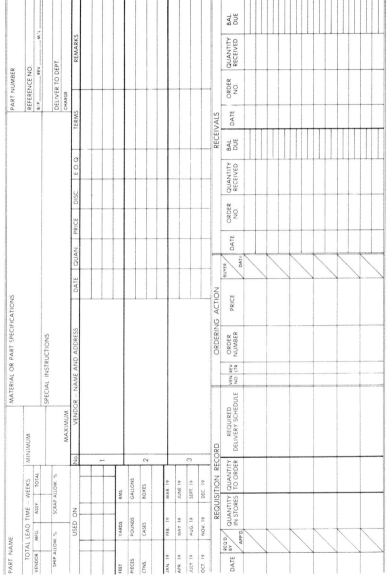

Fig. 11 Traveling requisition used by General Binding Corporation is typical of the request forms that shuttle back and forth between requisitioners and purchasing. Top of form contains basic information on the item it covers; middle section is for vendor data; bottom area records individual buying transactions.

name and address show through, TR's can be used with copiers to produce actual p.o. copies without typing.

In any case, whether you use TR's in a conventional mode or as part of an advanced systems approach, the handy forms will give a big lift to your buying efficiency.

11

REQUISITION/ORDERS SAVE EVERYBODY'S TIME

While the traveling requisitions discussed in the previous chapter trim paperwork on repetitive buys, one disadvantage is that they can't be used on one-shot purchases. As every buyer knows, one-time buys have a way of cropping up regularly in every purchasing department. (A v.p.'s secretary may need a non-standard office item; the maintenance department may require a special valve or fitting; etc.)

To handle such non-repetitive purchases under conventional systems, the buyer has to look each requisition over to make sure that its wording will make sense to the supplier. He may even edit the item description, so that it conforms to standard industry or trade terms. Then he adds data such as supplier's name, address and price, and turns the requisition over to purchasing's order typist.

Then—and this is the big kicker—the order typist dutifully transcribes the data from the requisition onto a p.o. form. And, in many cases, 90% of what she types is a direct duplication of what the requisitioner has already typed or handwritten on the requisition.

This is great practice for the order typist, but it's not very efficient in terms of work simplification. It's a direct violation of the systems theory that "one-write" methods are the best route to efficiency.

As a result, more and more firms (and this includes industry giants that have highly sophisticated EDP systems for repetitive purchases) are turning to requisition/orders to handle one-time needs that can't be anticipated.

Requisition/orders are designed so that the requisitioner prepares the bulk of the purchase order (quantity wanted, date needed, item description) as he writes the requisition. For this to happen, the requisition form must be laid out and constructed in one of three ways:

1. It may include a reproducing master of some sort (spirit duplicating or diazo) as one of its parts. With the master, purchasing can then run off as many copies as it requires: for the supplier, for receiving, for other departments, for file and follow-up, etc.

2. It may include a plain bond sheet that can similarly be reproduced on an office copier.

3. It may be a regular snapout form, with one sheet designated as the supplier's purchase order copy.

The advantage of the first two approaches is that they automatically provide extra copies that can be used for recording split shipments. But since running the copies is an extra step for the purchasing department—and since most one-time buys arrive in one shipment anyway—the third approach is the most popular.

In many companies, conventional requisitions include data that is more or less "confidential." This may include entries such as requisitioner's name (which, if the supplier finds it out, may spur him to back-door buying at the user level), and other internal entries regarding charge account numbers, etc. But, if a requisition/order is carefully designed, such information can be deleted from the supplier's purchase order copy of the form.

One way to do this is to construct the requisition/order with an extra-deep top stub on the first sheet, if that is to be the vendor's copy. In that space, most internal data can be entered. It will thus appear on interior parts of the set, but not on the original.

In addition, there is no law that says the vendor's purchase order copy has to be the first part of the set. If the form is set up so that the supplier gets one of the inside copies, the use of pattern or striped carbon preceding his copy will effectively mask out confidential internal entries.

An excellent example of this type of form is the requisition/order used by The Upjohn Co. Illustrated in Fig. 12 is the top copy of this form, which is a five-part snapout set.

In using the form, the requisitioner fills out all the data that he would normally enter on a conventional requisition: quantity and date needed, item description, etc. He even has a space (upper right) where he can enter the name and address of a "suggested supplier."

The buyer processes this form just as he would any other requisition: adding the chosen supplier's name (in the section reading "For Purchasing Use Only"), price, etc.

Then, when the form is burst apart, the second copy becomes a complete purchase order, ready for mailing to the supplier—and prepared without typing.

The reason is that pattern carbon preceding the second copy prevents entries in the following sections from being reproduced: suggested supplier's name, follow-up date, and price. The same holds true for all entries below the item description section, *except* the "deliver to" location and "purchasing approval" block. At the same time, the second copy is printed with a few lines of text that do not appear on the top copy: a heading reading "Purchase Order"; Upjohn's name, address and company logotype; and standard packing/shipping instructions.

The big advantage of requisition/orders is that they eliminate repetitive retyping for the order typist. But there are also ways in which they can be big time-savers for the buyer.

For example, many companies construct their requisition/order sets so that they include not only a purchase order copy for the selected supplier but one or more extra sheets that can be used as quote requests.

This saves the buyer the chore of writing a letter or making a phone call to check prices and availabilities. He simply mails off the quote requests, after entering the names of the bidders he chooses. (This saves the order typist's time, too.) Then, when the proposals come back, the buyer just adds the successful bidder's name to the p.o. copy. At this point the order is complete and ready to be mailed out.

It's true that the buyer still has to look incoming requisition/orders over carefully, just as he does conventional requisitions, to see if they make sense. But, when requisitioners know that the entries they make are going to go direct to the supplier as part of the p.o., they're more likely to take extra pains in preparing requisition/order forms. This is basically a matter of education, and it's easy to print a few lines of "instructions" on the top of each requisition/order form. Such instructions can point out that the form should be typed or legibly handwritten with sufficient pressure to carbonize through all parts of the snapout set.

89903
REQ. NO.

PURCHASE REQUISITION ORDER

FOR PURCHASING

USE ONLY

PURCHASE ORDER
NO. _____

SUGGESTED SUPPLIER

STREET

| CITY | STATE | ZIP CODE |

DISTRIBUTION:
WHITE
WHITE — TO PURCHASING EXCEPT CAPITAL ITEMS:
BLUE — SEND TO PROPERTY
CANARY — ACCOUNTING.
PINK — RETAINED BY REQUISITIONER

(for Purchasing use only)

DATE	SHIP DATE		FOLLOW-UP DATE
QUANTITY	ITEM	CATALOG NUMBER – DESCRIPTION	TOTAL PRICE

(This column for Purchasing use only)

☐ SUPPLIES   ☐ REPAIRS   ☐ INVENTORY   ☐ REPLACEMENT EQUIPMENT   ☐ NEW EQUIPMENT   ☐ MISC.

| EQUIPMENT NO. | EQUIPMENT CLASS |

REQND. DATE	DATE WANTED (SPECIFY DATE)	BY UNIT NO.	REQUISITIONED FOR	(FOR ORDERING UNIT REFERENCE ONLY)	WORK ORDER NO.
					C. R. NO.

Receiving Deliver To:

| ORGAN. UNIT NO. | BLDG. | FLOOR | PERSON: | JOB NO. | PROJECT NO. | AMOUNT BUDGETED | ACCOUNT NO. |

| REQUISITIONED BY | PHONE EXT. | APPROVED BY | APPROVED BY | TAX EXEMPT ☐ YES ☐ NO | PURCHASING APPROVAL |

Fig. 12 Requisition/order used by The Upjohn Co. is a five-part set. Top copy, shown here, is prepared by the requisitioner in normal fashion. After buyer's entries, the second copy of the set automatically becomes a complete purchase order, ready for mailing.

Some buyers may be reluctant to use requisition/order forms because so many requisitions are hand-prepared. They may feel that it's asking too much of a supplier to have him read handwritten orders. When you come right down to it, however, this is not very realistic thinking. Countless handwritten letters go through the U.S. mails every day—personal correspondence, letters to family and friends, social notes, etc. In most cases, the person getting such messages doesn't have any real trouble in reading and understanding them.

Some purchasing executives (perhaps your boss) may not like the idea of having "purchase orders" scattered throughout the plant at various using locations. He may prefer to have such documents under lock and key in the purchasing department.

Here again, however, this is not very realistic thinking. It's really nit-picking—since the requisitions do not become purchase orders until someone in purchasing signs them. This point can be prominently featured as part of the text on the purchase order copy. Or, if desired, purchasing can set up a system where the purchase order copies have to bear some sort of validating imprint before they become legal and binding commitments. The device used for the imprinting can be kept in purchasing, available only to authorized buying personnel.

What it all adds up to is that you don't have to have high-speed computers or other sophisticated hardware to shortcut the paperwork on one-shot buys. You can also do it with a well-designed requisition/order and a ballpoint pen.

12

DON'T SWEAT SMALL ORDERS

It doesn't take a Sherlock Holmes to spot the buyer who has never given any thought to ways of beating the small order problem. He's the buyer who is always on the phone, has the biggest pile of open requisitions on his desk, and signs more orders than anyone else in the department.

And, since he's so busy "putting out fires," he often thinks that he has no time to give to look-ahead systems of fire prevention.

The reason that many such buyers get into the paperwork trap in the first place is that they're too rigid in their thinking. They feel that every item the company needs—no matter how minor—has to be individually sourced, priced, ordered, received and billed. Or they may be forced into this attitude by an accounting department that demands a complete audit trail on every 79¢ purchase.

The reasoning goes something like this: you can't issue a check without an OK'd invoice, you can't OK an invoice without a receiving report, you can't have a receiving report without a purchase order, and you can't write a purchase order without a requisition.

The end result is that the buyer gets stuck with a ridiculous pile of paperwork.

The ironic thing about this approach to buying is that a good part of the paperwork is superfluous. There are simpler ways to handle the buying job without forfeiting controls. Most of these ways involve long-term agreements with selected suppliers—suppliers who can help the buyer lick his paperwork problems as well as get the goods in to the point of use.

Because a great deal has been written about this subject in recent years—with some companies developing their own terminology that isn't always 100% accurate—let's look for a minute at some of the terms that have been developed.

The first is "contract buying." As it's used for the most part today, this term describes a concept rather than a specific technique. It's a broad, general term that has come to cover just about all types of long-term agreements. Strictly speaking, the word "contract" should be limited to arrangements which include a firm commitment to buy. But, in present-day use, this distinction isn't often observed.

Another term that's common today is "blanket order." In many cases the term blanket order and contract are used interchangeably. A safer bet, however, is to limit the term blanket order to those agreements covering a broad family of related items. One rule of thumb is to look at it this way: A contract is an agreement under which items, quantities and prices are all specifically nailed down; a blanket order is an agreement where any one of these three factors may be left indefinite.

When you come right down to it, contracts and blanket orders represent the two main classes of purchase agreement that a buyer can negotiate for long-term needs. But there are three more terms that are increasingly being used in industry today, and it's important to know what they mean and how they work.

The first is "systems contracting."

In most cases, oddly enough, a systems contract is not a contract; it's a blanket order. It does not commit the buying company to buy a specific quantity of goods (although it may include a forecast of anticipated requirements).

The word "systems" in the phrase "systems contracting" has two connotations:

In the first place, it reflects the emphasis on mutually developed procedures that will simplify buying and selling for the supplier and the buyer. (Example: extensive use of multiple purpose forms, price catalogs, item specification sheets, Data-Phone and other electronic hook-ups, etc.)

In the second place, it indicates that the buyer is buying a complete package or system of the seller's technical know-how, back-up support, and administrative savvy.

The second term that's widely used today is "stockless purchasing." This simply means that the efficiencies of long-term agreements such as systems contracting (speedy deliveries, back-up stocks for non-standard items) enable the buyer to operate without inventory stocks. He depends on the supplier to serve as his stockroom, and to deliver the goods as they're called for.

The third term is "consignment buying." This refers to programs where the supplier maintains vendor-owned stocks right on the buyer's premises, paid for only as they're used.

No matter what type of long-term agreement you want to set up, it's a good bet to write the agreement on a regular purchase order form. This will give you the protection of your standard terms and conditions. (It's true that a very loosely worded blanket order may not be considered a legal contract when it's originally written, because it doesn't commit you to any particular quantity. But, if you have a release form referring back to the original order's terms, they will come into force when the release is made.)

In some cases you may be able to predict demand on an item, and set up a firm contract covering its purchase for whatever period you choose: six months, a year, or even two years. You can do this by making the firm quantity part of the agreement, or by setting up a so-called "requirements contract." (With a requirements contract, you guarantee to buy all or a specific percentage of your requirements for an item from a particular supplier. Since this type of contract is usually used on production goods—and since your company might want to start making some items in-house before the expiration of such a contract—the best bet is to use phrases such as "our *purchased* requirements" in wording the contract.)

The advantage of firm contracts is that they assure you of uninterrupted deliveries of goods. And, except for primary raw materials, you may be able to negotiate firm-price contracts that aren't subject to price escalation. In a rising market, this will be a cost advantage to your firm.

By listing firm prices on the contract, you also gain paperwork advantages. If you furnish accounting with a copy of the contract, you won't have to approve individual invoices. The accounts payable group will be able to handle that part of the paperwork.

You can gain the same paperwork advantage on blanket orders, where you haven't made a firm commitment to accept a given quantity of goods. Most suppliers will quote you a group of prices based on your estimates of demand (especially if your past estimates have been accurate) and you can make these prices part of the blanket order. If prices change during the life of the blanket order, you then have to notify accounting by means of a change notice or memo. But, just as with firm contracts, accounting can handle all the invoicing paperwork under such a set-up.

An alternative to listing flat prices for each item on a blanket order is to set up sliding price scales for the various materials covered. Under such a set-up, you might note that certain twist drills would be furnished at the following rates: 1–5 @ $1.05 ea.; 6–10 @ $.95 ea.; 11–20 @ $.85 ea.; etc.

An agreement worded in this way could also list surcharges that would apply if the vendor had to break a standard package in making a shipment. If accounting had a copy of the master agreement, it could again handle invoice-approval without bothering you or anyone else in purchasing.

Still another technique—one that's widely used on maintenance supplies and miscellaneous services—is to write a master agreement in general terms. Such an agreement might read something like this:

"This agreement to cover our requirements of . . . . supplies, to be released during the period . . . ."

As noted above, this agreement won't be a contract until you make a release. It also means that someone in purchasing will have to approve individual invoices. But it still opens the way to simplified methods for authorizing shipments and registering goods into the plant.

Wherever possible, these simplified methods should be based on having requisitioners or department heads make releases—notifying the buyer only after the fact.

Depending on circumstances, the using department can either telephone its releases to the supplier, chosen in advance by purchasing, or can use a special release form like the one illustrated in Fig. 13.

This form, which is typical of the ones widely used in industry today, is not only a "shipment release" but is also a "planning and commitment authorization." It spells out just how many items have been received so far against the master order, and authorizes the supplier to buy material for and fabricate a specific number of additional items. It even gives an estimate of what will be required in the future, to help the supplier in his production planning.

Although this form is designed for production-type goods, similar forms can easily be developed for the purchase of supplies and services. Every time someone else prepares and sends out such a form—whether it's material control, the stockroom or an individual requisitioner—the

**BLANKET
PURCHASE ORDER
RELEASE**

RELEASE NO.	DATE	BLANKET P.O. NO.	DATED	PART NO.	DRAWING NO.	REV.

**SHIPMENT RELEASE
PLANNING AND COMMITMENT AUTHORIZATION**

IMPORTANT

1. THIS RELEASE RELATES TO ALL TERMS, CONDITION OF SALE AND SPECIFICATIONS CONTAINED IN THE SUBJECT BLANKET ORDER.
2. NOTIFICATION OF SHIPMENTS, INABILITY TO SHIP OR INFORMATION REGARDING CUMULATIVE SHIPMENTS SHOULD BE SENT TO MATERIAL CONTROL DEPARTMENT AT ABOVE ADDRESS.
3. DO NOT, UNDER ANY CIRCUMSTANCES, OVERSHIP RELEASED QUANTITIES, AS SUCH OVERSHIPMENTS WILL BE RETURNED FOR CREDIT.
4. THE PURCHASE ORDER NUMBER, QUANTITY, PART NUMBER, REVISION NUMBER AND DATE OF MANUFACTURE MUST APPEAR ON ALL INVOICES, PACKING SLIPS AND CONTAINERS.
5. VENDOR'S RECEIPT OF THIS RELEASE WITHOUT EXCEPTION CONSTITUTES UNQUALIFIED ACCEPTANCE OF REVISED TOTAL COMMITMENTS.
6. SCHEDULE #2 IS TENTATIVE SCHEDULE FURNISHED FOR YOUR GUIDANCE ONLY. NO COMMITMENT IS EXTENDED FOR THESE ITEMS UNTIL THEY APPEAR IN SCHEDULE #1.

V
E
N
D
O
R

QTY. LAST REC.	DATE REC.	SECOND LAST QTY. REC.	DATE	TOTAL QTY. REC. AS OF THIS DATE — QUANTITY	DATE	QTY. PAST DUE

AFTER LAST SHIPMENT CONSIDERED FABRICATE AND SHIP AS SPECIFIED BELOW   SHIP ↑ THIS IMMEDIATELY

ARRIVAL DATE *	QUANTITIES	REMARKS
TOTAL SCHEDULE #1		

*NOTE: MUST BE AT OUR LOCATION BY DATE SPECIFIED.

SCHEDULE #2				

AUTHORIZED SIGNATURE

THIS AUTHORIZATION SUPERSEDES AND CANCELS ALL PREVIOUS AUTHORIZATIONS AGAINST PURCHASE ORDER INDICATED AND IS SUPPLIER'S AUTHORITY TO PURCHASE MATERIAL AND/OR FABRICATE AND SHIP AS SPECIFIED ABOVE.

ORIGINAL

VENDOR'S ACKNOWLEDGMENT
ACCEPTED SUBJECT ONLY TO THE TERMS AND CONDITIONS ON THIS RELEASE SCHEDULE AND NONE OTHER. WE WILL SHIP AS DIRECTED.
VENDOR
BY
TITLE   DATE

Fig. 13 Blanket order release form for production materials features section (Schedule #2) where supplier is advised of probable future requirements. Release forms for supplies and miscellaneous services may not be so comprehensive, but they still spare the buyer a great deal of unnecessary paperwork.

buyer is spared all the detail of sourcing, getting and comparing bids, approving the order, etc.

At the same time, the buyer doesn't lose control. He is the one who writes the original master agreement to begin with. Since he get copies of all the release forms (or incoming shipping papers on telephoned releases) he's constantly kept up to date on what's happening. Then, when the order is complete, he has a full record of everything that has come in against it. He can use this information when he renegotiates the agreement—which is the only time that really creative effort (as opposed to paper-pushing) is required.

Some buyers fail to use long-term agreements because they feel that individual sourcing—even on penny ante items—will get them better prices. But the shortsightedness of this approach can easily be demonstrated.

If a buyer makes $12,000 a year, and works a 35 hour week with two weeks vacation, his net worth to the company is better than 11¢ a minute. So, if he spends just five minutes getting a 50¢ lower price on an item, his big success will result in a 5¢ loss to his firm—not even counting the costs of typing a special order and accounting's costs in processing an individual invoice.

Don't sweat small orders; it's far better to play it cool with master agreements wherever you can.

13

TELEPHONE ORDERS AND OTHER SHORTCUTS

In addition to the long-term agreements discussed in the preceding chapter, there are any number of other systems that a buyer can develop to shortcut paperwork and give himself more time for creative buying.

Some of these systems may require the cooperation of suppliers. Others may need the help of requisitioners within the buying firm. But, whatever procedure is involved, the buyer must recognize the four essential elements of any purchasing transaction. These elements are:

(a) Identification of the buying company's needs;
(b) Communication of those needs to the supplier;
(c) Receipt of the material;
(d) Payment of the bill.

On the face of it, it might seem as though (b)—communication of buying needs to suppliers—was the only area directly concerning the buyer. In actual practice, however, it doesn't work out that way. It's often in the other areas that problems arise; problems that those directly concerned with the matter can resolve only by consulting with the buyer.

So, if you set up systems that streamline (a), (c) or (d)—or make for more accuracy in those areas—you'll be doing yourself a big favor.

Here's a brief rundown on 10 ways to make paperwork go more quickly or accurately from one end of the buying cycle to the other:

1. *Telephone orders.* Telephone orders can be used effectively on the miscellaneous supplies requirements that crop up in every company and in every plant. The buyer has to call one or more sources to find a supplier who has the item on hand. While he's on the phone, he can give the vendor a telephoned OK to ship the goods at the price specified. All he has to do is explain that there will *not* be a written confirmation of the order.

It's true that this puts the buyer in the position of doing business on the supplier's terms and conditions, but this really isn't that important in buying miscellaneous supplies. Warranties and guarantees, for example, aren't that vital in dealing with this kind of goods. And many suppliers are only too happy to handle the order in this way, because after-the-fact paperwork may simply confuse things at their end. (This is especially true of local industrial distributors, who are geared to handling small orders on a more or less rush basis.)

For such deals, all the buyer really needs in the way of purchasing paperwork is a purchase order log like that illustrated in Fig. 14. Such a log will tell him the date he placed the order, the order number, the requisitioner's name, the vendor's name, price, and a brief description of the material. If the buyer wants to, he can include a section that will indicate data on incoming shipments: date, receiving report or packing list number, etc.

To identify individual shipments under a telephone ordering system, the buyer can tell the supplier to mark the shipment with the requisition number, followed by the requisitioner's initials as a suffix. If he wants to keep telephone orders readily identifiable from regular purchase orders, he can use a prefix for all such orders: either "T" for telephoned, or "V" for verbal.

In many cases the buyer may also want to tell the supplier that a separate invoice won't be required—that his accounting department will consider the packing slip or other shipping papers an invoice, and will pay against them after the buyer has OK'd them for price.

2. *Self-invoicers.* Self-invoicers are special forms that the buying company furnishes to regular suppliers, often as part of a long-term purchasing agreement. When the buyer or other authorized individual phones a release to the supplier, the vendor's sales service group writes the order up on a self-invoicer form.

Typically, such forms are multiple-part, carbon-interleaved sets.

DATE	T-ORDER	REQ'D BY	VENDOR	MATERIAL	PRICE	INV. NO.	DATE	P/L NO.	DATE
10/15	T-495-JB	J. Brown	Harris	Grease	5-	29621	10/17	4321	10/16
10/15	T-385-RT	R. Towhe	Ajax	V-belt	12-	8657	10/18	967	10/17
10/16	T-231-PJ	P. Jones	Acme	Bearing	8-	34951	10/16	8421	10/16
10/16	T-622-LM	L. Marsh	Draper	Folders	4⁵⁰				
10/17	T-861-JB	S. Bowen	Ideal	Rock Salt	33-	86249	10/19	2234	10/18

Fig. 14 Purchase order registers, to keep track of requirements phoned to suppliers, needn't be elaborate. All that's required is a running record of what's in the works: dates, order numbers, prices, etc.

They provide copies for the supplier's file, for the buyer, and for packing list and invoice purposes.

In effect, self-invoicers represent a slightly more sophisticated approach to telephone orders. They give suppliers an easy means of writing up such orders. They eliminate the need for someone in purchasing or accounting to rubber-stamp packing lists with an "invoice" legend. All the paperwork is prepared at one writing, by the supplier.

Also, by standardizing the format of shipping documents, self-invoicers make things easier for the receiving department. The receiving clerk doesn't have to contend with a wide variety of packing lists: different sizes, layouts, etc.

3. *Self-ordering.* Once a buyer has negotiated a master agreement with a supplier, he can often obtain additional savings by having the supplier salesman keep track of inventory. This means letting the salesman go into the storage area where his goods are stocked, to determine when and how much to reorder.

To a buyer who's been raised on the philosophy that buyers and sellers should maintain an arm's length relationship, this may sound like heresy. But in actual practice there's much to recommend the idea.

The salesman, after all, is an expert on his commodity line. He can come up with many useful ideas on alternate products, pooled-order possibilities, etc. And, if he can survey the place where his goods are physically located, he's much more likely to develop such suggestions.

This doesn't mean that the buyer gives the salesman carte blanche to write his own ticket on reorder quantities. But it does mean that the buyer will seriously consider the *recommendations* that the salesman makes in this area—based on a personal scrutiny of the stockroom's shelves. (Example: A recommendation to stock up, if there's storage space available, on an item that's slated for a price increase in the near future.)

4. *Day-of-week ordering.* This is a system under which the buyer buys certain types of items on certain days of the week. He might want to make Monday the day for ordering pipe, valves and fittings; Tuesday the day for ordering electrical supplies; Wednesday the day for office items; etc.

Doing this automatically permits ganging or pooling of small requisitions into big orders, with a significant reduction in paperwork. The buyer simply holds all requisitions until the appropriate ordering day, and then consolidates them into worthwhile orders.

To make a go of this system the operating personnel in the various departments have to be alerted to how it works. They have to understand the purpose of the system, and the buyer must furnish them with a list of the days selected for the various classes of items. Otherwise, a constant stream of rush and emergency exceptions will make the procedure unworkable.

5. *Other pooling techniques.* Turning a host of picayune orders into larger orders is always a good technique for paperwork reduction— and there are other ways this can be done.

As noted in Chapter 10, it's possible to design traveling requisition forms with this thought in mind. Or, in companies with inventory control monitored by EDP, the computer can readily ascertain ganged-order possibilities. It can be programmed to kick out items *near* the reorder point at the same time it kicks out items actually at the reorder point within a certain class or family of commodities. Then the buyer, or the inventory control specialist, can decide whether such "can order" items should be added to the "must order" items on which purchase orders will be prepared.

Or, if a purchasing department doesn't have access to a computer within its own company, chances are that it can get all the benefits of EDP from one or more suppliers. More and more industrial distributors (who handle the nuisance items where purchasing paperwork really builds up) are offering their in-house EDP hardware and software capabilities to buyers, as an inducement to doing business with them. Some manufacturers are also getting into the act with this kind of "systems selling." For the buyer, it means a chance to use EDP to determine usage trends, spot standardization possibilities, and shortcut paperwork in many ways.

6. *Laundry lists.* Despite the banal-sounding name that's been applied to them, "laundry lists" are real time-savers for many buyers in all sorts of enterprises.

A laundry list is a purchase order—or requisition/order—covering goods or materials that are ordered time and again to the same specifications. To save time and effort, the item descriptions are printed on the forms, along with standard packaging specs. This means that the person filling out the order merely has to enter the quantities wanted in the box next to each item.

In addition to saving time for the buying company, laundry-list forms also make things easier for the supplier's sales service personnel.

7. *Check-attached orders.* To shortcut accounts payable's paperwork chores, it's possible to design a purchase order form that includes a voucher check for the supplier. The buyer signs the check as he signs the order—and further billing is eliminated.

Many systems are geared to having the buyer compute the exact amount of the total order, and enter it on the check portion. But more and more such systems are based on sending the supplier a blank check. The supplier then adds exact amounts for hard-to-figure-in-advance details such as freight charges, and fills in the amount of the check himself.

All companies using check-with-orders protect themselves by limiting the amount of such checks. The dollar limit is printed right on the face of the checks, making it impossible to "kite" them. But the amount of the dollar limit varies: from $25 to $100 and even up to $1,000.

In any event, since the systems get the money to work in the supplier's bank account with minimum delay, a buyer can often negotiate extra price advantages from the sources to which he sends check-with-orders.

8. *Petty cash.* There's nothing new about petty cash. It's been around, as a standard business practice, for years and years. But, unfortunately, some buyers feel that it's an admission of weakness if the petty cash fund is ever used for a conventional purchase. They prefer to write purchase orders even on cat-and-dog items that are readily obtainable at some local store.

A better approach is to be realistic about such local buys. Let the user make his own pick-ups on one-time needs where you don't have a master agreement with any source. Let him pay for them out of petty cash. This will speed things up for him, for you and for the supplier.

At the same time, you should have some running record of what is happening in (or to) the petty cash account. One way to accomplish this is to have purchasing (or your buying section) made responsible for replenishing petty cash funds. You can then insist that those using the fund present you with sales tickets or cash register slips. This gives you a chance to spot items and suppliers where long-term agreements can profitably be set up.

9. *C.o.d. shipments.* Collect-on-delivery shipments (usually used when a supplier isn't too sure of the buyer's credit rating) can also be used to shortcut accounts payable detail-work. Requisitioners can phone their needs to non-local suppliers, and stipulate c.o.d. shipment. Then, when the goods arrive, the receiving department can pay for them from a c.o.d. fund.

Like petty cash funds, c.o.d. funds should be under the buyer's control when it comes to replenishing the kitty. This gives the same control on out-of-town buys as the buyer gets on local petty cash purchases.

10. *Invoice OK's.* Last but not least, you can often save yourself a great deal of time by simply skipping the paperwork on confirming orders where someone in the company has engaged in back-door buying. Instead of preparing a formal order on such buys—just to get an accounting copy of the p.o. into existence, so the bill can be paid—get accounting to accept your signature on the invoice itself.

This doesn't mean that you should encourage or even condone back-door buying—a few remedies for which are suggested in Chapter 21. But it does mean that it's pointless to issue an order after the material has already been received, just to get the bill paid.

The important thing is that the buyer's signature is needed. Its immaterial whether it's on a p.o. form or on the invoice form that the supplier has submitted. If you want a copy for your files, just make a copy of the invoice after you've signed it. This copy can then be placed in the alphabetical file for closed purchase orders, and you have a near-complete record of the transaction. If you insist that the requisitioner tell you why he chose the supplier and agreed to the price, you can add his comments to the invoice to make a complete record.

14

SPECIAL FORMS FOR SPECIAL NEEDS

If you're a typical buyer—handling phone calls from countless outside suppliers and just about everybody in the company—you probably have had days when you'd like to have torn the phone out by the roots. That's what the buying game is all about: the simultaneous juggling of 1,001 projects ranging from open orders to cost estimates.

Every buyer has days like that. But, if *every* day finds you longing for some way to give your phone its final quietus—or of stemming the tide of visitors to your office—you're probably trying to handle too many communications on a personal basis.

As noted in previous chapters in this section, there are occasions when the immediacy of a personal interview is vital in resolving a communication problem. There are other instances where, since a phone call has to be made anyway, you can use the same call to avoid subsequent paperwork. But there are many routine communications that a buyer gets involved in every day, that can most effectively be handled by special forms.

It may sound like a contradiction in terms to recommend more paperwork as a means of work-simplification. In today's business world, many executives look on the word "form" with as much distaste as they do other more pungent four-letter words. But in the final analysis you can't get away from the fact that a well-designed form is still the fastest, easiest and most accurate way of recording and transmitting information. (Even computers, the whiz-kids of the information-processing game, become more efficient when they're fed forms that can be optically "read" by machines as well as by humans.)

If you're still dubious, consider the alternatives that are available when you want to transmit an item of information, or request that data be submitted to you. There are just four:

1. You can arrange a personal meeting with the individual in question.

2. You can write him a letter, memo or telegram.

3. You can telephone him (which may involve busy-signal delays, long waits while his secretary locates him, call-backs, etc.).

4. You can jot a few entries down on a form and shoot it off to him in a matter of seconds. And, in cases where you're asking for information, you can usually set the form up so that the recipient can also use it for relaying the data back to you.

If you are developing a tin ear from the pressure of your phone receiver, right now is the time to make a wholesale study of your communication needs and patterns. The purpose of the study should be to identify any phone calls (and personal visits) that could be handled by means of a special form.

A good starting point for such a study is to keep a log for a while, on which you can record the salient facts about incoming and outgoing phone calls. Like the one illustrated in Fig. 15, such a log doesn't have to be elaborate. A few headings on the top of an 8½ x 11 ruled pad will do fine. This informal register should indicate the people who are calling you, and whom you're calling, plus a very brief description of the purpose of each call.

After you've built up sufficient information on the register sheet, you can study it to spot cases where you're (a) constantly getting the same type of phone calls, or (b) making the same type of calls with similar frequency.

Depending on circumstances, it shouldn't take you more than a week or two of recording phone calls before you have enough data to indicate trends. The only thing you have to look out for is timing; it wouldn't be a good idea to schedule the telephone-call logging for a period involving unusual activities. Example: end-of-year inventory pe-

Date	Call From	Department	Call To	Department	Purpose
6-17	J. Brown	Acctn'g			Order complete?
"	P. Smith	Engin.			Wanted catalog
"	H. Nye	Stores			Expedite order
"			F. Green	Engin.	Get add'tl B/P's
"			M. Watt	Mfg.	Clarify specs

Fig. 15 Register sheet for incoming and outgoing telephone calls will give the buyer an indication of the people with whom he's constantly handling matters by phone. It will also indicate the nature of the calls, and pinpoint cases where forms can effectively replace phone messages.

riods, weeks smack in the middle of capital equipment or construction programs, etc. Such special activities could give you a mis-reading on the type of calls you're ordinarily engaged in. (On the other hand, there's no reason why you can't repeat a call-logging program six months or so after you first give it a try.)

When you look over the call-record sheet, you'll probably find many instances where incoming phone calls could be handled with an existing form. When this is the case, it's a signal that some of the people you're dealing with need a gentle nudge. They need to be reminded that the forms are available (either from your office or the stockroom) and that they should be using them for all but the most urgent communications.

More importantly, as far as systems refinements are concerned, your analysis of the call-record sheet will show you the types of communication where new forms can be designed as time-saving aids.

Suppose that your analysis of outgoing calls shows that you're spending an inordinate amount of time negotiating delivery dates with requisitioners. Suppliers may not be able to hit the delivery dates originally requested on requisitions, meaning that you have to call the requisitioners back to find out just what shipping dates are acceptable to them. Or, in many cases, suppliers may be unable to meet their promised delivery dates after they've received purchase orders from you.

In either event, straightening out such problems can eat up a great deal of telephone time. But a simple form such as that illustrated in Fig. 16 will give you a handy means of notifying requisitioners of delivery problems without tying you up on the phone. The requisitioners, in turn, can use the form to let you know whether the late delivery will be acceptable, or if other action will be necessary.

(Needless to say, you have to have enough time to send forms such as these through the internal mail—and to get your replies by mail, too. This is one reason why stockroom areas and other requisitioning sources should be kept posted on lead times in general. If every requisition is so urgent that it *has* to be handled by phone, you'll never get off the phone.)

Perhaps you don't want to go to the extent of running a full-scale survey on your incoming and outgoing phone calls. (That's your prerogative. But just don't kid yourself that you "don't have time" for such a study.) If you do feel this way, an alternate approach is to skip the call-registering routine, and to go directly to identifying the people and departments with whom you're in constant communication. Often you can get a head start on identifying such contacts simply by analyzing the nature of your company's business or product line.

It goes without saying that any buyer spends a lot of time on the phone with suppliers and with other departments directly concerned with procurement: the stockroom, material or production control, receiving, accounts payable, etc. The same holds true for intra-departmental communications with the head of purchasing, with other buyers, with expediters, and with order-typists and clerks.

But, if you're in a technically oriented company, you may also be spending a great deal of time thrashing matters out with staff members in engineering, design, manufacturing or quality control. Or, in a job shop environment, much of your internal communications may be with marketing, estimating, or cost accounting.

Whatever approach you take to identifying the sources for and recipients of repetitive-type information, you'll undoubtedly find many cases where a form can replace phone calls and personal visits. (You may also find situations where a simpler version of an existing form can be used to good advantage. Fig. 17, for example, illustrates a price change slip that's barely 3″ x 5″. When sent direct to accounting by the buyer, such a chit can eliminate the need for formal typing of a multi-part purchase order change notice.)

As you make increasing use of forms to handle routine communications, the number of phone calls and personal visits you have to handle will drop. In addition, as far as forms replacing phone messages is con-

TO: _____   DATE: _____

FROM: _PURCHASING DEP'T_____   DATED_____

RE REQUISITION NO.: _____   SUPPLIER: _____

P.O. # _____ ITEM NO. _____   THEIR SCHED. _____

DELIVERY REQUESTED: _____   _____

CHECK ONE AND RETURN TO PURCHASING DEPT.

Cancel & Reorder Other Source

Hold & Reorder Other Source

Their Delivery Date O.K.

Order Substitute Material, Req. Attached

SIGNED: _____   APP'D BY: _____

REMARKS:

Fig. 16 Advising requisitioners of suppliers' delivery dates—often a time-consuming process involving long waits and call-backs—can readily be handled with simple forms like this one.

PRICE CHANGE REPORT

P.O. No.	Part No.

Placed At: Unit Cost

Change To: Unit Cost

Remarks:

Date / / /   BUYER

Fig. 17 Study of routine communications may also disclose cases where complex forms can be replaced by simpler ones. Example: this price change report which takes the place of formal p.o. change notices.

cerned, both you and those you deal with will gain accuracy. This is an advantage you should stress if you meet resistance to the use of forms in place of phone calls.

Depending on circumstances, some of the forms you need may require multiple distribution. One way to get around this problem is the purchase of blank snapout sets, imprinted as needed.

In other cases, home-made forms produced on duplicators and copiers can readily be developed to plug the communications loop-holes that so often exist in procurement systems.

The next and final chapter is this section on back-up aids and simplified systems will discuss some of the proven methods for do-it-yourself forms design.

15

DO–IT–YOURSELF FORMS DESIGN

Once you've decided that there are specific forms that would help you in the day-to-day communications that are part of your buying job, the next step is to design the forms. And, to be sure that the forms will add as much efficiency as possible to your communication systems, you've got to understand a few points about forms design.

This isn't as difficult as it sounds. Although whole books have been written on the subject, there are really just three points that you have to keep in mind:

1. A well-designed form is one that is easy for the originator to fill in.

2. A well-designed form is one that is easy for the recipient to take data from.

3. A well-designed form is one than can economically be produced, and readily filed for reference if need be.

Just about all the other guidelines for good forms design stem from these three concepts.

To make forms easy for originators and recipients to use, you have to consider the documents that may exist on either side of the form in question, in the systems-chronology. You have to lay the new form out so that, as much as possible, it follows the same pattern of entries as the one before it and the one after it. A classic example of this is where a basically common format is used on requisitions, bid requests, purchase orders, change notices and receiving reports. The job of extracting data from one form and putting it on another—whether it's an order typist working from requisition to purchase order, or a receiving clerk working from p.o. to receiving report—is vastly simplified.

By the same token you can, by sticking to standard sizes wherever possible, assure that forms can be economically produced and easily filed.

After you have isolated the function that you want your new form to handle, your next step is to consider how the form should be printed or reproduced. Depending on how fully equipped your in-plant reproduction department is, you will probably have several options. One choice is to prepare some sort of master—mimeograph, hectograph (spirit duplicating) or diazo (whiteprint)—or to use in-plant offset or high-speed electrostatic units to run the form. Or, for forms that you know will be long-run, you may want to have them printed by an outside commercial source.

Most of the forms you develop will be short-run—at least at first. For one thing, you may want to experiment with the use of the form to begin with, before you finally settle on its final format.

When this is the case, you will probably start out by designing the form on a typewriter. There is nothing wrong with this technique, as many excellent forms can be laid out for internal use by a skilled typist. But—and this is a big but—you do have to be careful when using this method. If the typist doesn't know her stuff, the result can be a forms-design abomination.

Take a look at the form illustrated in Fig. 18. This form (presumably) isn't being used anywhere, as it was pecked out by the author solely as an example. But it does show two of the main dangers that you have to look out for when using a typewriter as a forms design instrument.

In the first place, the amount of space allocated for the various entries is completely cock-eyed. There is more space allowed for short entries (digits for telephone extension, order numbers, etc.) than there is for long entries such as material description. This danger is especially common on typewriter-prepared forms layouts because a typewriter is relatively inflexible in its spacing mechanism. A pica machine spaces 10

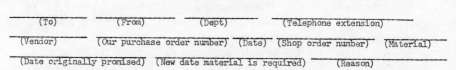

Fig. 18 Dangers of using a typewriter as forms design instrument are illustrated in this hypothetical "expediting request." Amount of space allocated for various entries isn't proportionate to the length of the entries; user can't readily determine where the first entry should be placed.

characters to the inch horizontally, and an elite model spaces 12 characters.

In the second place, the person making out this form would have to stop—prior to making the first entry—to determine where that first entry should go. Above the line? Below the line? The only way to tell, really, is to look down to the very bottom of the form to get a "fix." On a short form such as the one illustrated, that may not be a big problem. But on a long, deep form, it's a real time-waster.

One way to solve this particular problem is to put all typed headings (abbreviated where possible) at the beginning of the space for entries—and then follow up with the underscore key. Or, if you want to, you can consider using some of the more professional forms design techniques that are applied by big-company forms control staffs and commercial printers. (In some cases, as will be noted later, you can use such methods even on forms that will be reproduced internally on simple copying equipment.)

The starting point for professional forms design is a forms layout sheet. These sheets, which just about any rotary forms printer will supply you free of charge, are marked off with grid-lines so that measuring character-spaces becomes a snap. You can readily gauge the amount of space you're using on each line.

Fig. 19 shows how such a sheet might be used in redesigning the expediting request previously illustrated in Fig. 18. The layout sheet used in this case is a standard 1/6" (vertical) by 1/10" (horizontal) grid. And here are a few steps to keep in mind when you're using layout sheets such as these:

1. Determine the size form you need (preferably a standard).

2. Using a ruler and a medium-hard pencil, rule the outer dimensions of the form.

3. If the form is going to be commercially printed on rotary equipment, leave 1/4" margins on either edge. The rotary press needs this "gripper" space.

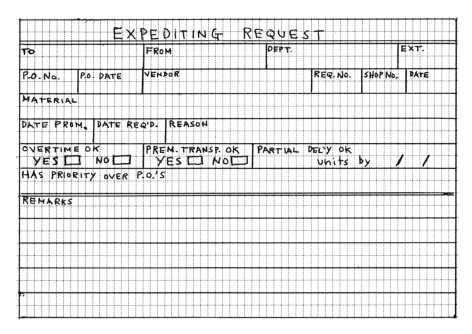

Fig. 19 Forms layout sheets make it easy to lay out well-designed forms. Grid-lines on the sheet give the designer guide marks he can use in establishing vertical and horizontal spacing. In many cases, such layout sheets can be used for forms to be reproduced on standard, office-type duplicating equipment.

4. Neatly print the headings you want, following the same order as other forms in the system. You don't have to limit yourself to one character per space on the grid, but print as compactly as you can. Using all capitals is best.

5. Put the headings in the upper left corner of a box for each entry. This allows more space for the subsequent entries. It also avoids any ambiguity as to where the entries are to go.

6. Space the lines vertically based on the method that will be used in filling out the form. If you are positive that the form will always be prepared by hand, you can make the vertical spacing 1/4". But if it will sometimes be typed, use three-to-the-inch spacing (two 1/6's). This allows space for either hand or double-spaced typed entries.

7. Especially for typed forms, line up as many headings as you can. This will let the typist make the best use of her tabulator stops in filling out the form.

8. Use ballot boxes wherever possible, where the person filling out the form can simply enter an "X" or a checkmark.

9. Use double rules to segregate various areas of the form, where appropriate.

10. For sections that you know will be prepared by typewriter, *don't* include horizontal "leader lines" as guides. They're not necessary, and do more harm than good in such cases.

If you follow these 10 rules, you should wind up with a first-class form on the layout sheet. Then, when you present it to a commercial printer, his composition job will be that much easier. He'll have something definite to work with, the job will go faster, and you won't have to pay him for forms design work—whether he lists such charges separately, or tries to bury them in his over-all price.

The same advantages hold true when you turn such a forms design layout over to an in-plant offset print shop. The company employee who handles composition will know exactly what you want, and will be guided accordingly.

In addition, there may be cases where you can use your layout as artwork for forms to be produced by hectograph or electrostatic duplicators. Although the masters for such reproduction are traditionally prepared by typewriter, it might be possible to go to a hand-drawn master.

To do this, simply get a good calligrapher to re-draw your layout on whatever type of master is necessary. A draftsman from the engineering department could probably do the job in nothing flat.

The end result of this process will be blank forms with all the headings hand-drawn. This may sound unprofessional, but it really doesn't matter on internal forms, anyway. Also, if a form is to be filled out later by typewriter, the use of hand-drawn headings can actually be an advantage. It makes the subsequent entries (typed) stand out more vividly.

Specialists in forms control and design work claim that the cost of processing forms runs up to 20 times the cost of the forms, in some cases. This may be an exaggeration, but there's no denying that the labor cost of pushing paperwork is tremendous in all organizations. If you can make your special, in-plant forms easy to work with, you'll be doing yourself and everyone else in the procurement cycle a big favor.

PART THREE

Purchasing Communications

When a breakdown in communications occurs at any level of any organization, nothing but trouble results. This is true whether the organization is a family suffering a generation gap between parents and teen-
agers, or a government plagued by credibility gaps between its agencies
and the taxpayers. It takes people to staff and run organizations, and it
takes open lines of communication for people to work together har-
moniously and effectively.

To take this general principle one step further, the most efficient
purchasing department is one that functions as a message center rather
than just a paper-processing point. The head of the department realizes
that purchasing is a profit-making endeavor—not a reactive operation
through which requisitions are tidily turned into orders. He expects his
buyers to be innovators, seekers and experimenters. He also expects
them to be skilled at interpreting any data they find in their challenges
to the status quo—and at relaying their findings internally to other departments and externally to suppliers.

In such a department, the buyer has to be a skilled communicator simply to keep up with what the boss expects of him. And even in less dynamic departments, where performance standards may not be so high, the buyer should make every effort to improve his communications methods and techniques.

(Doing so will at least relieve some of the tedium that probably goes with such a dull buying job. It will also work to the buyer's long-term personal advantage if he ever changes jobs or gets a new hot-shot purchasing manager as boss in his present company.)

There are many types of information that a buyer has to pass along in the course of doing a first-rate purchasing job. They include technical, financial, economic and other matters: availability of new processes and materials, potential suppliers' credit standings, market analyses, world trade and export/import studies, etc. But, every time the buyer transmits a communication on any subject, it is to people that he directs his messages. It is people that must understand the message—and, in many cases, to be moved to action by it.

The chapters in the following section, therefore, describe various ways in which proven communication methods can be applied to typical situations within the purchasing environment.

16

PURCHASING NEWSLETTERS PAY OFF

A purchasing newsletter is just about the easiest way to improve purchasing communications within a company. A good newsletter circulated to using departments will inevitably improve relations with them. And, for multi-plant firms, an intra-departmental newsletter will give various buying groups a means to share their knowledge, pool their purchasing experience, and exchange valuable information.

The buyer's role in publication of a newsletter will vary. In some companies, the editing of the newsletter may be rotated among buyers. If so, the buyer had better prepare himself for the day when he is tapped for this assignment. In other firms, the purchasing agent may handle the editor's job himself. But even if this is the case, the buyer has a responsibility to feed the P.A. the news items that are worthy of publication.

Whether as editor or reporter, the buyer has an important stake in any purchasing department newsletter. He should be familiar with the basic purpose of the newsletter—and should be able to relate this objective to the publication's contents, format, frequency and distribution.

Since any publication must be geared to the interests of its readers, the contents of a newsletter will depend largely on its audience.

If, for example, a newsletter is to be circulated to operating groups, the items published should be related to requisitioners' information needs. Typically, these would include current lead time data, technical commodity rundowns, market developments, notes on the availability of new manufacturing or finishing processes, comments on specialty suppliers' capabilities, and brief explanations of purchasing systems.

It's especially important to include data on purchasing systems when a new or revised buying method is being set up. If requisitioners get an explanation of the "why" as well as the "how" of new techniques—such as Data-Phone, systems contracting, etc.—they'll be more receptive to the changes that the systems may impose on their own departmental routines and policies.

Purchasing newsletters circulated within the buying organization, on the other hand, should be keyed to the interests of plant buyers or other purchasing staffers.

Such a newsletter can therefore be more detailed in its treatment of new buying methods being tested. It should also discuss new products, report value analysis and standardization case histories, and outline other cost-cutting techniques. In addition, it should provide a sounding-board for the exchange of information on vendors' quality, service and manufacturing capabilities and should call attention to news or systems items printed in local or national publications.

Some internal newsletters also include book reviews of new purchasing texts, and any literature particularly pertinent to the company's industry or product line.

As a result, a purchasing newsletter will serve as a supplement to the department's policies/procedures manual. It can be used to publicize topical information that doesn't warrant permanent reference, and to re-emphasize important data on a timely basis.

(Typical example: restatement of purchasing's policy on refusal of Christmas gifts. This subject would make a good topic—for either an internal or external newsletter—sometime in October or November.)

It's also important, for either type of newsletter, to personalize the contents as much as possible. This means giving bylines to contributors (whether they're purchasing staffers or "guest columnists" from other departments), and making sure that cost reduction ideas are credited to those responsible for the suggestions.

As far as format goes, letterhead size is a good bet, because 8½″ x 11″ sheets can easily be filed if a reader wants to save various issues of a newsletter. Use of standard-size sheets also makes it easy to run the newsletter on whatever duplicating equipment is available—hectograph, mimeograph, or offset.

More important than sheet size or duplicating method, however, is the trick of making a newsletter interesting and easy to read—and physical layout will often contribute to readability.

Arranging the typed matter in two columns rather than one is a good idea. So is the use of colored paper, short paragraphs, capital letters or underlines on key phrases, the letter-spacing of headlines.

In addition, if a newsletter editor wants to dress up his material at little extra cost, he can have it reproduced on stock promotional-type letterheads. These letterheads are available off-the-shelf from commercial sources, and are colorfully illustrated to punch up any type of message.

How often a newsletter should be issued will depend on the local situation. But—although some purchasing departments publish newsletters on an irregular, as-needed basis—the best approach is to have some specific frequency for publication. In general, this should be at least quarterly and (except for special issues to cover problem situations) not more often than monthly.

In any event, the first issue of a newsletter should start off with an announcement of the publication's purpose and expected frequency. It should also outline the mechanics of submitting material, and should point out that such submissions are welcome.

How widely a purchasing newsletter is distributed is also pretty much a matter of individual choice. But even when a newsletter is primarily for intra-department use, it's a good idea to send courtesy copies to other department heads. By the same token, at least a review copy of an external newsletter should be circulated within the purchasing department.

Each individual getting the newsletter should also know who else in his organization receives it. This helps each recipient determine how extensively he should reroute the newsletter within his own group. One way to do this is to print the complete distribution list on the reverse side of one page.

An example of an intra-purchasing newsletter that has met with considerable success is a quarterly one issued from the home office of a company with several plants and other installations around the company. Here's some of the material that the newsletter has carried in the past:

— A note that plant purchasing agents might want to pass *Purchasing Magazine's* lead time reports along to operating foremen;

— An outline of a new expediting method;

— An explanation of the Defense Materials System and its impact on the company;

— A discussion of trade relations *vs* reciprocity;

— A recap of upcoming labor negotiations in various industries;

— A rundown on the perils of single-sourcing;

— A case history on how the traffic department helped the purchasing group locate hard-to-find spare parts for railroad cars.

The editor of this newsletter says that the publication has succeeded because it is keyed to local purchasing interests, and because submissions from the field are encouraged.

In recent issues the newsletter has included a regular "Transportation Briefs" column, authored by the traffic department to help all members of purchasing in their buying jobs.

All told, a purchasing newsletter is one of the most valuable investments in time that a purchasing department can make. It may not win the P.A. or buyer a Pulitzer prize—but it will certainly give a big lift to buying efficiency.

17

THE BUYER AS PUBLIC RELATIONS MAN

Every buyer should view himself as a public relations representative for his company and for purchasing.

This doesn't mean that he should try to assume the flash and dash of a Hollywood press agent, whose main forte is hard-selling the client. But it does mean that the buyer should constantly strive to project a favorable image of his firm and of his profession.

The best way for a buyer to do this is to project a favorable image of himself—in his dealings with salesmen, with production and technical personnel inside and outside the company, and with the public at large.

The buyer is in an enviable position for this type of p.r. activity because purchasing is a "people business."

To prove this, just compare the buying job with other duties within a company. Engineers and other technical personnel are primarily concerned with equipment, materials, or processes. Financial men are interested mainly in the collection, coordination and control of accounting data. Even personnel specialists, although their main job is working with people, are for the most part limited to dealings within the company.

Purchasing, on the other hand, is in constant contact with officials from other firms, as well as with staffers from internal departments. Buyers' opportunities for fruitful public relations work are limited only by their willingness to polish their p.r. skills.

For, when you come right down to it, each buyer represents his department. The department, in turn, represents the company to outsiders —and the purchasing profession to all other employees except salesmen.

Should the buyer make a big deal out of the fact that his p.r. "audience" is made up of two groups—those inside and outside the firm? Not at all. Good public relations techniques are good no matter whom they're aimed at. If the buyer cultivates these techniques across the board, he's bound to improve the impression that he makes on other people in both areas.

As a practical matter, however, the buyer may want to concentrate on improving "external" public relations. For there are certain complications and complexities—the whole question of business ethics, for example—that don't arise in interdepartmental relationships.

For the buyer, this means demonstrating that his firm is a good one to have as a customer. (His general attitude will also reveal a great deal about the company's personnel policies and practices—but this is secondary to the prime area of buyer-seller dealings.)

If the buyer is to portray his company as a good customer, his daily dealings with actual and prospective suppliers must be characterized by many personal attributes. The buyer must show that he is honest, capable, thorough, courteous, dependable, responsible, enthusiastic and articulate.

This list of desirable traits isn't just a modified version of the Boy Scout oath. Although the characteristics listed are necessarily general, there are specific ways in which they can be applied to the purchasing field.

Honesty: It goes without saying that a reputation for honesty and integrity is absolutely essential. The buyer must be above suspicion, and all his dealings with suppliers must be conducted on a high ethical level.

In practical terms, this means that the buyer should refuse any gifts other than inexpensive advertising give-aways, should pick up his fair share of luncheon tabs, and should scrupulously avoid any partisanship in selecting suppliers.

In addition, the buyer should honor the confidential nature of any information that suppliers give him. This is especially important where vendors' prices or state-of-the-art manufacturing techniques are involved.

Ability: Technical ability is an important part of a buyer's capacity to present a favorable image. Nobody likes to do business with someone who doesn't understand the field under discussion. Such a situation (you may have faced it in sessions with new salesmen or requisitioners) invariably makes it more difficult to come to a "meeting of the minds."

As a result, the buyer should seek to become an expert on the commodities he handles, should bone up on new items that may be assigned to him, and should also become familiar with business law and trade customs governing the products he buys.

Thoroughness: Closely allied to the question of ability is that of thoroughness—or, if you will, of "persistence."

The persistent buyer is one who never fails to do his homework prior to an important interview, who is painstaking in gathering background material for negotiation sessions, and who is diligent in all research activities.

Sometimes, even an extremely "capable" buyer may not have all the facts and figures at his disposal when he's face-to-face with the seller. The "thorough" buyer always has them ready.

Courtesy: A little courtesy goes a long way—and nowhere is it more important than in buyer-seller relationships.

In this area, courtesy means that the buyer sees all legitimate visitors promptly, and gives them his undivided attention during each interview.

Promptness in receiving visitors, however, is only part of the story. The buyer should also be prompt in returning phone calls, answering letters, acknowledging bids or cost reduction suggestions, and notifying unsuccessful bidders.

Moreover, since the very nature of the buyer's job forces him to say "no" more often than "yes," he should practice tact and diplomacy in doing so.

Dependability: The dependable buyer is one whose word is as good as his bond, and one to whom suppliers can look for support in all areas of buyer-seller relationships.

Closely allied with honesty and integrity, dependability is nevertheless a trait worthy of discussion in its own right. For while an "honest" buyer may observe the highest standards of ethical behavior, it often takes a "dependable" buyer to back the supplier up when he needs help.

Seeing to it that vendors' cost reduction suggestions are given fair and impartial testing by operating departments is the type of job where a buyer can demonstrate his dependability.

Responsibility: The other side of the coin, as far as working with suppliers is concerned, is responsibility. The buyer must remember that "the buck stops here"—on his desk.

It's often tempting to blame other departments for inadequate lead times, extremely rigorous quality standards, or rejection of value analysis suggestions proposed by suppliers.

But, in the final analysis, vocal recriminations against other departments will simply tarnish the p.r. image of the company as a whole.

The buyer should stand up for his vendors' rights—but he should also accept the rap when things don't work out exactly to suppliers' liking.

Enthusiasm: If a buyer isn't enthusiastic about his company and his job, he might as well forget about brightening up the p.r. image of his firm.

Enthusiasm, after all, is the salesman's stock in trade. If it's not matched by equal zeal on the part of the buyer, there is no chance of forging a working rapport between the two men.

The buyer, in other words, should be excited about the unlimited opportunities he has to cut costs, improve product design, reduce inventory, or otherwise heighten efficiency.

And, if the buyer stresses the team approach in talking to salesmen about such improvements, he will spark even more enthusiasm from them.

Communications: Since public relations is essentially a matter of communications, the buyer must be able to articulate and demonstrate the standards and ideals that he subscribes to.

To do so, the buyer must understand the importance of personal neatness and good grooming. He must also recognize the value of poise— as shown by such little things as a firm handshake or the practice of telephone etiquette.

Finally, the p.r.-minded buyer must cultivate his writing skills, to make sure that all his correspondence is to the point without being pedantic, brief without being curt, and—above all—free of pomposity or stuffiness.

18

HOW TO WRITE A REPORT

Every buyer should cultivate the ability to write clear and concise reports. If he does, he'll not only improve purchasing efficiency, he'll also show that he can organize his thoughts and present them effectively.

Report-writing skill is especially important in purchasing. The reason is that the department's activities are broad-scope. It wouldn't be unusual for a buyer to have several reports to prepare in a single day. These might include an activity summary covering his commodities and purchases, a market study, a technical development survey, an award justification, or results of a field trip.

Some reports cover relatively simple subjects. Others are more complex. But there are five steps to follow in preparing any report. These are:

1. Determine the purpose of the report;
2. Collect the material;
3. Organize the material;
4. Write the report;
5. Edit it.

Determine the report's purpose: The easiest way to nail down the purpose or purposes of a report is for the buyer to ask himself a series of questions about it. These might include:

Who requested the report? What use will he make of it? Does he need it for immediate decision-making, or for future reference? Will the requestor be the only one to read the report, or will he circulate it? Who will be the pass-along readers, if there are any? Other buyers? Personnel in other departments? Members of management? What interest will these other readers have in the report?

Much the same questions should be asked about unsolicited reports —those that the buyer prepares on his own hook. In either case, the questions should be aimed at probing the *ultimate* purpose of the report. This will help pinpoint whether the report should be simply a compilation of facts or opinion supported by facts.

Collect the material: For long-term projects, where the buyer has plenty of time to gather material, the first step should be to set up a subject folder. Then, after he has identified his sources for information, the buyer can use the folder to store his material.

This material will probably include clippings, memos, tearsheets and random thoughts that the buyer jots down as they occur to him. Three-by-five cards are good for notes like this, because they're easy to reshuffle into an orderly pattern later.

This is important because the buyer shouldn't be too selective during the "collecting material" step. He should gather all material that seems pertinent to the subject. It's better to wind up with too much material—which can be distilled during organization, writing and editing— than it is to have too little material.

For other reports, especially those covering specific meetings or other events, the buyer will have to cultivate his note-taking skill. This is a matter of practice. Here are just a few hints on the mechanics of note-taking:

Use a fairly large note pad—preferably 8½″ x 11″, and certainly no smaller than a stenographic pad. Use check-marks, stars or other designs to flag comments needing further explanation. If speech texts are furnished in advance, underline key phrases as the speaker reads them. Don't get too far ahead of the speaker, as he may ad-lib. Transcribe your notes as soon as possible.

Organize the material: A well-organized report is one that follows a logical, orderly pattern. The buyer must first look at all the material he has collected. Then he must classify the raw facts by category. Finally, he must decide on the most appropriate order in which to present the categories.

An outline will help, and the key point to remember in drafting an outline is the "purpose" of the report. If the purpose is to present an opinion or recommendation, this statement should be the number-one topic in the outline. Then, step-by-step, the rest of the report should support the statement.

(Typical example: a report on whether or not a new vendor should be added to the approved-source list. Such a report should start off with the buyer's opinion on this matter—and should then tell why the buyer feels that way.)

Many reports are combinations of narrative comments and statistical references. In such cases the best bet is to extract all statistics and put them in a separate section or appendix. This makes it easier to read the narrative text straight through. It's an especially useful technique when the statistics—new vendors' equipment lists, for example—can be used for permanent reference after the report has served its basic purpose.

Some reports, especially annual reports covering purchasing activity on many commodities, can't be handled in this manner. A good alternative is to set up a standard pattern for presenting data on each commodity or other subject. For purchased goods, this might include total annual usage, plants or departments using the item, and year-ago and current prices. Then, in separate "remarks" at the end of each section, the buyer can comment briefly on outstanding developments such as technical developments, new sources coming on stream, etc.

Often, a standard form can be used to cover all aspects of such reports.

Write the report: If the buyer knows the purpose of his report, and has collected and organized his material well, writing the report is easy. All he has to do is put himself in his reader's shoes, and follow the outline as he tells himself all about it.

This identification with the reader is the key trick of any kind of writing. As part of this identification, the buyer should make every effort to keep words and sentences short. One way to check how he's doing on this score is to use the "fog index" test.

Developed by writing consultant Robert Gunning,[1] the fog index measures the complexity of written material in terms of word and sentence length. Here's how to apply the index:

First, take a sample passage of at least 100 words. Find the average number of words per sentence. (Independent clauses—those that

[1] *How to Take the Fog Out of Writing,* The Dartnell Corp., Chicago, 1964

could stand alone grammatically—count as separate sentences.)

Second, count the number of three-syllable or longer words per 100 words. (Don't count: capitalized words; combinations of short, easy words; verbs made three syllables by adding "ed" or "es.")

Finally, add the two factors—average sentence length and percent of long words. Multiply this total by 0.4. Round off to the nearest whole number. The result is the fog index of the passage tested. The higher the index, the more difficult the passage is for the reader to wade through.

According to Gunning, the fog index represents the number of years' schooling that a reader must have to read the material with ease. A fog index of 10 can easily be handled by someone with two years of high school; a fog index of 16 means that it takes a college diploma to get the message from the text.

The fog index, of course, shouldn't be taken as a be-all or end-all in judging the readability of writing. (At the extreme, it could lead to Dick-and-Jane type reports reading like this: "ABC Co. is a supplier. It is a good supplier. It is in Akron. Akron is in Ohio. I went to Akron. I saw ABC's equipment. It is good equipment . . .")

On the other hand, the fog index is an excellent way to spot two of the most common errors in all business writing: run-on sentences, and too many jaw-breaking words.

Other common errors that report-writers should avoid include jargon, ambiguous phrases like "sagging markets," and pseudo-technical expressions. Watch out for "parameters," "interfaces," "orders of magnitude"—and words ending in "ize" or "ation."

Edit the report: The basic purpose of editing a report is to insure that it's accurate, tightly written, and clear to the reader.

This means that the editor is the reader's representative, not the writer's. And this is why newspapers, magazines and other publications have editors to look over authors' work before it's set in type.

For the buyer who has written a report, this practice has much to recommend it. If he turns his report over to another buyer, and asks for frank comments on it, he'll get an objective, third-party opinion. This opinion will help him spot cases where his writing has been ambiguous, over-long, or poorly organized.

In some cases, the buyer may not be able to solicit third-party comments before turning his report in. If so, his own self-editing should be just as tough and dispassionate as he can make it. One way to achieve this objectivity is to set the report aside for a few days after it's been drafted, before the final version is edited and typed. Such a cooling-off period can often be very helpful.

19

INFORMAL CORRESPONDENCE GETS RESULTS

Right now is the time to put on a campaign to cultivate an easy informality in your business correspondence. If you do, you'll reap several important benefits:

First, you'll save yourself a lot of time.

Second, your individual letters and memos will be more likely to get the desired results.

Third, you'll project a better image of yourself in general. You'll avoid the risk of sounding like a stuffed shirt.

Fourth, you'll set the tone for the replies that you get back from your readers. With any luck, they'll reciprocate in kind. If they do, both you and they will have taken a step toward stemming the torrent of gobbledygook that characterizes so much business writing today.

This last point is extremely important. The current sorry state of business correspondence is due mainly to the effect of stiff, formal writing. The big companies that do a lot of government business have picked up "bureaucratese" and have converted it to "corporationese." The smaller firms that work with the larger ones, often as suppliers, have been impelled to follow suit.

It takes a certain amount of guts to buck the trend. If you get a letter referring to "cognizant personnel," the easiest way out is to use the same phrase in your reply—or, perhaps, to make some reference to "jurisdictional authority." (And all the time, of course, what you and your correspondent really mean is "the guy who's in charge.")

As a buyer, you have a built-in advantage when it comes to corresponding with suppliers. You're the customer. You can call the shots in determining how formal—or informal—your correspondence is to be. It'd be a pretty stupid salesman or sales manager who'd complain that your letters were too flip. So, even if you can't practice informality in internal company communications—although it might not be a bad idea to try it—you can certainly do so with your suppliers.

Some buyers may find it difficult to do this. They're accustomed to the precise, legalistic terminology of purchase orders and contracts— and they may have trouble shifting gears in their writing styles. (By its very nature, legal writing has to be somewhat formal—although not nearly so much so as some lawyers and courts make it.)

This doesn't mean that there's a distinct line separating formal and informal writing. Instead, the question is essentially a matter of tone and style—and the general effect on the reader. To determine this in advance, there are certain things you can look for:

1. An informal letter is a personal one. The reader gets the impression that the writer is addressing him as an individual, not just as a representative of a company.

2. An informal letter uses a conversational style. It simulates a face-to-face meeting between the writer and the reader. (If you find it difficult to make your letters sound like this—and many businessmen do—try to imagine the reader sitting across the desk from you as you dictate.)

3. An informal letter is brief and to the point. It's straightforward. It gets to the heart of the issue quickly, without restating obvious historical background material. It highlights various matters in the order of their importance.

4. An informal letter stresses the active, rather than the passive voice. (Compare "We liked your idea," with "Your idea was liked by us.")

5. An informal letter uses short, everyday words: "method" instead of "methodology," "visit" instead of "visitation," etc.

6. An informal letter uses short sentences—and short paragraphs.

(Even short, punchy sentences *look* forbidding if they're jammed together in solid blocks.)

7. An informal letter will be spiced with a bit of humor when appropriate—perhaps in the form of contemporary slang or catch-phrases. But don't put quotes around the phrases. It will make them look "corny."

8. An informal letter is one that has plenty of you's and yourses in it. ("Thank *you* for *your* suggestion that . . ."; "We appreciate *your* interest in. . . .")

If you make a conscious effort to give your business letter a more informal tone, you'll probably succeed. And, if you take a sampling of your letters at six months' intervals or so, you'll be able to review them and note your progress.

But—simultaneously with your efforts to keep the *content* of your letters informal—you should also take steps to simplify the *mechanics* of your correspondence. By doing so, you'll save yourself a lot of time. And by encouraging your suppliers to use similar short-cut correspondence systems, you'll probably get faster answers back from them, too. The trick here is to write as few letters as possible, and to keep them as short as possible. There are many ways to accomplish this.

Suppose that your engineering department is preparing a list of specifications for a new job. Under a formal correspondence system, you might incorporate the specs into the text of inquiry letters to several suppliers. Under a less formal approach, you could simply ask engineering to type the specs with plenty of carbon copies. Then you could attach the copies to very brief transmittal letters. Or if you only had one set of specs to work with, you could make copies on an office copier.

With an office copier you can make duplicates of incoming letters from suppliers—and of handwritten replies that you make on the margins or bottom. Under this system, the supplier gets his original back with your notation, and you keep the reproduced copy for your file. In addition to saving time, the method reduces the number of file cabinets you need for your correspondence.

You can also use handwritten reply memos for outgoing correspondence. Most stationery stores stock three-part carbon-interleaved sets designed just for this purpose, and you can easily have them imprinted with your company's name and address, or even your own name and location.

Finally, you can just attach one of your business cards—perhaps with a brief note jotted on it—to much of the material you mail out to vendors. There's no reason why you can't use this approach in forwarding copies of prints, drawings, parts lists, or other self-explanatory material.

If you do use your calling card as a transmittal slip, however, be sure to put your correspondent's full name somewhere on it. In big companies, all mail is opened in the mail room. If you don't have some identification other than your own on the piece you mail, you may wind up getting it back again by return mail.

20

KEEP REQUISITIONERS ON THE BALL

Whose fault is it when a requisitioner submits a requisition with a vague or impossible delivery requirement, with an incomplete item description, or with other vital data garbled?

One answer—and it's a tempting one for any buyer who gets such a requisition—is that the blame lies squarely with the requisitioner.

But the truth is that educating requisitioners is one of the most important parts of a buyer's job. If a buyer shirks this responsibility, he'll wind up spending more and more time with requisitioners. Instead of being free to concentrate on important matters, he'll be tied up explaining the routines of how to make out requisitions.

Typically, this may involve pointing out that delivery dates like "As soon as possible" or "Rush" don't give the buyer any real information to work on; that quantities requested solely as "boxes" or "packages" can easily be mis-interpreted; that item descriptions should be as complete as possible—or even that authorization signatures should be legible.

This doesn't mean that a buyer shouldn't explain such matters to his requisitioners. He very definitely must do so—and that is what requisitioner education is all about. The point is that the buyer should only have to explain such matters once.

Things usually work that way when traveling requisitions are used. The buyer edits the TR the first time he gets it, and from then on there aren't any problems.

With one-time requisitions, however, it's a different story. Anyone and everyone in the company uses these forms to originate requests for goods and services. Quite often, it's someone new to the company that makes out the form. So requisitioner education on a continuing basis is a must.

This is especially true if a firm is considering the use of the combination requisition/orders mentioned in Chapter 11. If a user can't phrase his requests correctly without buyer assistance, he's a poor risk to prepare forms that will be relayed straight to the supplier without interim order-typing.

To remedy the situation, the buyer needs his boss's help and cooperation. So, if a buyer is plagued with incomplete or otherwise incorrect requisitions, his first step should be to keep track of the errors and inconsistencies he has to cope with. He might want to record the individuals or departments that are giving him the most trouble, and list the most common problems.

With this information, the purchasing manager may decide to issue a general memo to all department heads, asking them to have their staffs reread certain portions of the purchasing manual, if there is one. Or, if the department issues a purchasing newsletter, the P.A. may want to devote an issue to tips on preparing requisitions correctly. Current lead times might also be published in this way.

Another solution to the problem is to redesign the requisition form so that it includes instructions on how it should be prepared. Again, this requires the cooperation of the purchasing head who authorizes such printings. But—especially if all the buyers in a department are being deluged with incorrect requisitions—the P.A. will probably be willing to consider such forms redesign. (One selling tool that any buyer can use in proposing such a plan is to point out that many government forms do include step-by-step instructions. Examples: drivers' licenses and car registration forms, in many states.)

If a company's requisition forms are printed on rotary presses (and most multi-part forms are), complete instructions can readily be added to the reverse side at little cost. Since rotary presses can print both sides of a sheet in one pass, the only real expenses are for one-time composition and platemaking.

At the same time, there are several ways to add efficiency to the front side of requisition forms. One way is to outline the areas that the requisitioner is to fill in, with bold lines. Another way is to use screened (shaded) tint blocks on those areas of the form.

Even on his own there are various steps a buyer can take to get requisitioners on the ball and keep them there.

One approach is to be a little more hardnosed about accepting requisitions that aren't properly prepared. If the buyer bounces a few requisitions back to the originator for explanation of inconsistencies, this will make it clear that he doesn't have a crystal ball on his desk. Or, if he prefers, the buyer can send requisitioners a note asking for more information.

In either case, the point is to put the requisitioner on notice that nothing is going to happen to his request until he clarifies it. And doing this will often straighten out some of the chronic offenders whose errors are due more to laziness than to ignorance.

Another useful trick is to make maximum educational use of the p.o. copy that is sent to requisitioners after an order has been typed. To highlight the manner in which an original requisition has been edited within purchasing, the buyer might want to rubber-stamp this copy when appropriate.

Typically, the stamp might read "Please note the correct commercial nomenclature of item _____ on this requisition," or "Please note the corrections made on this request."

No matter what the wording on the stamp, it should also suggest that the requisitioner save the p.o. copy for reference in preparing future requests.

The buyer should also make every effort to get basic information about his commodities out to the people who use them and requisition them. This could be in the form of a general letter or memo to all users, listing the specifications and characteristics of various materials and supplies.

An alternate approach would be to provide the stockroom with educational material of this sort. Since most requisitioners go first to the stockroom to see if the items they need are stocked, the stockroom manager is in an excellent position to help the buyer get accurate and complete requisitions.

Suppose that your company stocks just a few types of paper for general office use. Invariably, some secretaries and clerks will need special papers for special jobs. And the odds are that they don't have any idea of the specifications that apply to paper in general: sheet size, weight, grade, type, color, grain direction, etc.

But if your stockroom manager had a sample packet of various non-stocked papers available from suppliers—plus a list of all the above specs—he could give requisitioners real guidance in making out their non-standard requests. And you, in turn, would perhaps be spared the job of figuring out what a requisition for "six packages of mauve paper" really meant.

The same principles of requisitioner education apply, whether a buyer handles raw materials or maintenance supplies. A long-term training effort will invariably cut down on the amount of day-to-day coaching that a buyer has to dispense to users.

21

HOW TO CLOSE THE BACK DOOR

Back-door buying is a problem that affects all buyers. No matter what commodity a buyer handles, he will always have to contend with self-styled procurement experts from operating departments.

Engineers often try to by-pass the buyer in the purchase of fabricated parts. Office managers and systems men do the same thing on office equipment and printed forms. Advertising managers feel they are uniquely qualified to buy promotional literature and artwork. Maintenance foremen share the same conviction about MRO supplies.

If a buyer accepts all these users' claims that their items are "special," he'll wind up with nothing to buy. His position will be reduced to that of a clerk. He'll spend his time pushing paperwork —and his company will lose all the advantages of professional purchasing.

Every buyer thus has an important and personal stake in combating back-door buying. Even in strong purchasing departments—where the P.A. has evolved a written statement of purchasing's authority and responsibilities—the buyer must constantly demonstrate that he is best fitted to do the buying job.

There are two reasons for this. First, a written statement of policy is worthless if it isn't backed up by deeds. Second, personnel changes in operating departments often bring in people who are unfamiliar with centralized purchasing.

Suppose that a new design engineer joins the company. It's quite possible that he may have done some buying in his former job—either formally or informally.

In such a case, the buyer will be making a serious mistake if he assumes that the new engineer will automatically conform to company policy on vendor contacts. Instead, the buyer should take the initiative. The first time the engineer calls a supplier in for direct consultation, the buyer should tactfully remind him that such visits inhibit purchasing efficiency.

It's not always easy for a buyer to insist on his purchasing prerogatives. It's especially difficult when no written policy exists—or when the requisitioner is a department head or executive who outranks the buyer. But if a buyer makes a conscious and unremitting effort to oppose backdoor buying, he will generally be successful in the long run.

The first step in combating back-door buying is to understand *why* requisitioners try to handle their own purchases.

More often than not, they do so because of a lack of knowledge, emotional reasons, or a combination of the two.

In many cases, requisitioners may simply be unaware of purchasing's mandate to handle all purchases for the company. (As noted, this is often the case with new employees.)

Another problem is that requisitioners may mistrust the buyer's technical knowledge. Having worked out the design details of the item to be bought, they may hesitate to give the responsibility for procurement to someone else.

On the emotional level, the buyer often has to face hostility caused by the requisitioner's resentment, arrogance, fear or lack of self-confidence. (In many instances, a requisitioner's insistence on dealing with a certain supplier is a sign that he is over-dependent on the vendor for technical help. He needs someone to do his job for him.)

The buyer's second step in fighting back-door buying, then, should be to determine which of these reasons is behind each user's attempts to circumvent purchasing channels. And—although each case of back-door buying is different—the buyer's efforts to "sell" purchasing should be slanted to a common theme: the fact that centralized purchasing reduces costs, promotes efficiency, and improves suppliers' over-all quality and service.

The buyer should constantly point out that only purchasing has company-wide knowledge of vendors' facilities, abilities, current workloads, pricing structures, delivery performance and quality records.

One way to demonstrate the advantage of purchasing's handling all commitments is to pose a hypothetical case of what can happen when requisitioners deal direct with suppliers.

Suppose that the buyer learns that the head of the manufacturing department has called in a salesman from the ABC Co. In talking to the manufacturing manager, the buyer might say something like this:

"Charlie, you know and I know that ABC is a good supplier. I can understand your wanting to talk to them. But—just to show you what can happen when you call somebody in without checking with purchasing first—let me tell you a little story.

"You know the big order you have with the XYZ Co.? The one where we're having such a terrible time getting delivery? Last Tuesday I told them that they'd never get another order out of us unless they got the stuff to us on time. Then yesterday I learned that Dave, over in engineering, was going to call XYZ. He was going to promise them all the business on the J-10 project.

"What do you think, Charlie? Should I just sit tight while Dave makes the call? Or should I remind him—just like I'm reminding you— that all vendor contacts should be made through purchasing?"

In addition, there are many other ways in which a buyer can meet the back-door buying problem. Here's a checklist of just 10 basic approaches:

1. Keep a careful record of cases where back-door buying has resulted in poor quality, late delivery, excessive cost or other inefficiencies.

2. Drill suppliers on the need to check with purchasing before visiting requisitioners.

3. Set up a system for feeding information on new products and processes to requisitioners—promptly, accurately, and completely.

4. Don't hesitate to accept and process "tough" requisitions— those where it's difficult to locate a qualified supplier. Such requisitions may in effect be trial balloons sent up by users to test your sourcing skills.

5. Build up your technical know-how on the items you handle— by quizzing suppliers, visiting vendors' plants, attending seminars and trade shows, etc.

6. Insist that sample orders and trial lots of material be routed

INTERVIEW REPORT

To: Purchasing Dept. Attn.:		From: (Name and Dept.)		Date
Supplier's name		Salesman's name		Order no.
Length of interview	Initial visit? Yes☐ No☐	Arranged by purchasing? Yes☐ No☐	Product demonstration? Yes☐ No☐	Project no.
Other depts. at interview: (List)				
Purpose of interview				
Results of interview				
			Signature	

Fig. 20 Interview report, to be filled out by requisitioners after consultations with supplier representatives, will keep buyer posted on the details of such meetings. One way to authenticate such reports is to give similar forms to salesmen and insist that they submit separate reports on sessions with using departments.

through the receiving room—and that receiving notify you of all such receipts.

7. Process requisitions promptly, to avoid the possibility of users claiming that "purchasing takes too long to get the orders out."

8. Give credit to requisitioners who have assisted purchasing (through channels) in locating new supply sources.

9. Use a form, such as that illustrated in Fig. 20, to get prompt feedback on the results of users' interviews with supplier representatives.

10. Delegate routine releases against blanket orders and other long-term agreements to using departments. This practice will give requisitioners a sense of participation without forfeiting purchasing's control —and will give you more time to function as a strong buyer in other areas.

If you make your plans carefully, there's no reason why you can't close the back door without getting your foot caught in it.

22

STAY FRIENDLY WITH YOUR SALES FORCE

Whether you're a buyer for a job shop or a production-line plant, for a big firm or a small company, you ought to be on good terms with everybody in your sales department.

This doesn't mean that you should let your marketing executives lead you by the nose—telling you where to buy or how to apportion the business based on suppliers' sales volume as customers. That's reciprocity—and in many cases it's illegal because it is a violation of the anti-trust laws.

On the other hand, there are many instances where a free-and-easy, open relationship between purchasing and sales can offer mutual advantages to both groups.

Look at it this way. As a buyer, you certainly ought to know your company's business. If you don't know who your company's customers are, and the techniques that your sales staff uses in filling their requirements, then you're unaware of a key factor in your firm's operations.

Here's a rundown on some of the advantages you can *get* from working closely with your own company's salesmen, and on ways to make the most of such opportunities:

1. Your salesmen undoubtedly call on a broad variety of other firms, and are probably on a first-name basis with many of their purchasing agents and buyers. This means that you can ask them to pick up samples of any printed materials that other purchasing groups are currently using. This material might include external (and possibly internal) newsletters, welcome booklets, manuals, pamphlets explaining quality control or Zero Defects efforts, letters soliciting suppliers' help in value analysis and value engineering, etc.

It's true that you can also collect such samples from your own purchasing acquaintances or associations. But the more such material you collect, the more complete your files will be. And this will help you when you want to see how your own literature for suppliers stacks up against that of other purchasing groups. It will be especially helpful if you should want to prepare a new booklet or pamphlet that your company has never used before.

Even more important, you can ask your salesmen what they think of the material they collect for you. They'll be candid when they give you their opinions, because they won't have any ax to grind. They won't have to pull their punches at all.

This means you may get comments like this: "The P.A. over at ABC Co. thinks this letter soliciting our VA help is the greatest thing since 'Gone With the Wind.' But it leaves me cold because. . . ."

Then, if your salesman tells you precisely why it leaves him cold, you'll have a pretty good idea of the pitfalls to avoid when you next write a similar letter to your suppliers.

2. Over and above the tangible materials that your salesmen can collect for you, they can also give you a general insight into sales-oriented problems. In particular, they can fill you in on what they think of various customers' purchasing policies.

To sound them out on this, ask them how they rate their customers in their own minds. Perhaps they won't want to name names. But get them to give you a general rundown on their biggest beefs. What bothers them? Is it too many rush deliveries? Lack of appreciation for special efforts? Too many cases where orders aren't forthcoming after the salesman has spent days on design work for the customer?

Answers to questions like these—coming from a sales pro—can be invaluable to you in framing your own supplier relations policies.

3. Your company's salesmen can also give you a big assist by bringing back news of purchasing procedures that their customers have developed.

These procedures might be designed to shortcut paperwork, reduce the small-order problem, or solve any one of the bugaboos that plague both buyers and sellers in today's business world.

In many cases you may be able to use similar systems in your own buying work. But again, the salesman's comments will give you a frank opinion on the workability of such systems from the supplier's viewpoint.

4. In many of the customer firms your salesmen call on, there may be buyers who are specialists in certain commodities. This is especially true of big firms consuming large quantities of primary raw materials: ferrous and non-ferrous metals, chemicals, plastics, etc.

Such buyers are experts on market trends, pricing patterns, shifts in world trade policies affecting their items, etc. And, because these matters are so impòrtant to them, they may discuss them with your salesmen simply as topics of general interest.

In turn, if your salesmen feed such information back to you, you may be able to use it in your own buying decisions. It may give you an early warning on upcoming material shortages that haven't yet been publicized through the trade press and other conventional media.

5. In addition to gleaning as much data as possible from your field salesmen, you should also work closely with the groups that support the sales effort.

Advertising and sales promotion staffs are groups that can be of particular help. By giving purchasing notice of upcoming campaigns to increase sales, they can tip off big increases in material demand that might otherwise catch you unaware.

In addition, the inside sales service desk can corroborate field salesmen's comments—pro or con—about the paperwork buying procedures used by various customers.

By the same token, here are a few ways you can *give* assistance to the sales force:

1. You can provide factual information on material costs. (If your firm is a job shop, you may be doing this as part of your formal job duties.)

2. You can help the sales staff meet competitive-price situations, by suggesting alternate materials, manufacturing processes, and other cost-reduction ideas on specific end products.

3. You can give your salesmen tips on how you have simplified your own buying job with special systems. Let them have samples of your forms, booklets or other items. Have them take them back to their customers, just as they have taken samples of customers' materials back to you. Especially in smaller firms—where the purchasing agent may be handling several jobs, and doesn't have time to develop systems refine-

ments—your firm's customers will appreciate this thoughtfulness.

4. Most important of all, you can be of tremendous assistance in your company's efforts to train its salesmen.

In some companies, new salesmen spend a full week or two in the purchasing department as part of their indoctrination. In other companies, they may just spend half a day with the purchasing manager or with senior buyers. Or, in other cases, the purchasing head or one of his top aides may address a group meeting of several neophyte salesmen.

If your firm does ask you to help in training salesmen, go at it with all the enthusiasm you can muster. And, if it doesn't, you might at least ask the new man to lunch a couple of times, as part of a crash course to give him a few insights into purchasing.

Whether on a formal or informal basis, you're in the best possible position to tell him what his customers will expect of him. Tell him how you rate your suppliers. Spell out how important quality, service, price and technical assistance are to your (and his) firm. Outline purchasing policies in detail, and give specific examples of how you apply them in your buying jobs.

When you're through with this kind of discussion, your salesman should be a better salesman. And you should be a better buyer.

23

FORECASTS AND FUTURES

If your boss came to you and asked you what your most important commodity was, chances are you wouldn't have any trouble at all in answering him. You'd be able to rattle off the name of the item, the types or shapes you buy it in—plus a complete rundown on major suppliers, their prices, shipping points, etc.

But suppose your boss came to you and asked what would probably be your most important commodity five years from now. Would you be able to give him a reply based on facts?

Perhaps your boss will never come to you with such a question. But that doesn't matter. As a buyer, you should be an expert on the items you buy—and that means knowing what's probably going to happen in the future, as well as what has happened in the past. With this kind of knowledge, you can pass along significant facts to anyone else in the company who might be able to use them. In short, you'll be a forecaster—just as much as the company president, the board of directors, or any hot-shot economic counselors that they hire from the outside.

In many cases, in fact, you'll be in a better position to dig up pertinent data than the highest-priced consultant or economist. Reason: You're on the firing line where markets are made and trading patterns are established—not perched in an ivory tower. You're a participant, not a spectator. You share the action, instead of reading about it in a textbook on economics.

Here are some of the areas you can cover as forecaster for your firm:

Materials: This is an especially important area for manufacturing companies, since raw materials account for such a large percentage of total costs.

In this area, you should be on the lookout for new materials that are being developed at the research stage, for new applications for existing materials, and for combination materials such as clad metals and other composites.

Manufacturing processes: As far as production methods are concerned, there are two angles you have to consider. First, you have to keep an eye out for new processes that your suppliers might be able to use in producing purchased goods for you. Second, you have to weigh the possibility of using the new processes in-house on purchased materials.

In either case you have to consider many points, such as process speeds, economy, and tolerances. (Examples: Will advances in cold-heading give the same tolerances as machining? Will casting developments surpass traditional specification-limits of weldments or forgings?)

Market trends: In addition to technical matters such as materials and manufacturing processes, there are many other angles you have to explore—and market trends is high on the list.

In this area, you should look for new suppliers entering the market, for expansion or curtailment of existing suppliers' production facilities—and for any situations that might result in material shortages. And, if you do forecast a shortage of a material that's important to your firm, you should also be able to pinpoint what can be done about the situation: long-term contracts to sew up your fair share of what's available, development of substitute and alternate materials, etc.

Pricing patterns: You should also be able to predict, with at least some accuracy, what's going to happen to prices on the materials, parts or components you buy.

To some extent, this part of your forecasting will be closely related to market trends. For example, if a great many new sources enter the market, prices may stay the same or drop, because of heightened competition. Or, if many current sources get out of the market, prices may rise if demand outpaces supply.

There may be other cases where prices drop not so much because of competitive economic forces, as because of manufacturing improvements that increase production efficiency. In any case, you should be able to forecast the probable trend of prices on the items you buy.

Distribution methods: No matter what your commodities are, you should recognize that the cost of moving them to your plant represents a big percentage of their total cost. This means that you have to keep up to date on changing developments in traffic and physical distribution.

Typical questions in this area might include these: What transportation modes are now being used on my major commodities? Rail? Truck? Air? Water? Who are the major carriers? Where are they located and what geographic areas do they serve?

How about new sources? Are there carriers now capable of serving the new sources' plants? Will the new sources offer enough business to attract new carriers?

How about physical changes in the commodity? Will slight design changes in the product or its packaging permit containerization? Could raw materials possibly be pumped through pipelines—either as-is, in semi-solid states, or as slurries?

Services: Since the typical purchasing department buys services as well as physical goods, your informal forecasting efforts should also include a look at services. Ask yourself what services you are buying now, and what changes you can logically anticipate. Who will the new suppliers be? What services will they offer? How competitive will the marketplace for services be?

With services representing an ever-greater percentage of the country's Gross National Product, this is an area you can't overlook.

Legislation: From your contacts in the field, you may be able to come up with more precise legal information on your commodities than a battery of lawyers.

Suppose you handle your company's lease arrangements on various types of capital equipment. The salesmen and officers of the leasing firms can undoubtedly give you the word on upcoming legislation that might affect the tax breaks on rented equipment.

World situation: As a specialist on the items you buy, you should also be able to measure the impact of outside forces, worldwide, on price, availability, etc.

This means keeping up with tariffs, imposition of export/import quotas, trade wars and hot conflicts and skirmishes all over the globe. If any of these might have an effect on the items you buy, it is something you must be concerned with.

To do a really effective forecasting job, you have to work like a detective or a cryptographer—picking up different bits of information and fitting them together to come up with an over-all answer. It isn't easy. But—especially when you have just a few commodities for which you're responsible—you should be able to develop fairly accurate forecasts. You can then present the information either to your supervisor, or directly to those who have an interest in it.

Short-term, your forecasts of the availability of new materials might impel your company's production people to take an interested look at new capital equipment for processing such material. Or, long-term, your comments on the market might persuade your top management to start up production on a new product where the competition isn't too intense.

So, whether you present them now and then during the year or consolidate them in a year-end report, the forecasts that you make as a buyer can have a big effect on your firm's future as a profit-making company.

24

GET INTO YOUR PLANT

The biggest mistake any buyer can make is to spend eight hours a day polishing his chair with the seat of his pants. Immobility is a luxury buyers can't afford—not if they want to be idea-men rather than order-placers.

There are several reasons why it's especially important for buyers to get out into the shop, where the action is. They are related to the nature of the buying job—a slot that involves many different commodities, many different people, and many different plant areas.

The storeroom head or the production manager, for example, may scream bloody murder about monumental foul-ups. But "nuisance" problems that may be sapping efficiency at many different work stations often go unreported even by the employee who's experiencing the difficulty.

Examples: a V-belt whose chattering has increased so slowly that its noise hasn't been noticed even by the man standing next to it; a sticky valve that takes just a few extra foot-pounds to turn on and off.

If the buyer never gets out in the plant, he won't be aware of such situations. But if the buyer makes it a practice to spend some time out in the plant, he can be the problem-solver who squelches nuisance situations before they become critical.

Ideally, the buyer should be on a first-name basis with everyone who uses any of the items he buys. If he is, here's what will happen:

— By cultivating users' friendship, the buyer will be assured of candid comments when he asks their opinion on different products, materials and processes. If he wants to run in-house testing programs on new items, he'll get the cooperation he needs for this kind of work.

— Armed with the data he accumulates at the source, the buyer can apply his commodity know-how to finding better ways of doing things. If necessary, he can call in a salesman for specialized advice. In either case, he will start the corrective action *by defining the problem from the user's viewpoint.*

— As he comes up with more and more solutions to everyday problems, the buyer will gain the respect as well as the friendship of plant workers. They'll think of him as an idea man as well as a nice guy. They'll be even more likely to turn to him for advice and assistance. The entire effort to increase in-plant efficiency will snowball.

The best way to start such a program is to think of the materials cycle as involving three stages: procurement, storage/distribution, and use. Then, as he spends time out in the shop, the buyer can look for possible improvements in each of these areas.

In the area of procurement, the buyer might make it a point to ask shop workers what they think of different suppliers' quality and service. The man who uses the material is obviously in an excellent position to report on quality. He can also pinpoint just how helpful different suppliers' salesmen are when it comes to providing technical assistance, handling emergency requirements, suggesting alternate products, etc.

This kind of grass-roots input on supplier service is especially important when the buyer has negotiated blanket orders or contracts where releases are made by the requisitioner. It helps to keep the supplier salesman honest when he opens contract re-negotiation by claiming what a great job he's done in servicing the account.

The shop worker can also give the buyer valuable advice on how releasing and receiving arrangements for such contracts can be improved. Or, if such systems aren't already in use, the plant employee's viewpoints should be considered when the buyer starts thinking of such plans

In the area of storage/distribution, the buyer should be on the lookout for any situations where stock-keeping or disbursement methods cause inefficiency or inconvenience. A flagrant example of this would be if shop workers had to walk inordinate distances to get frequently needed materials or supplies. In other cases the buyer may have to do some detective work—and ask a few questions—to uncover situations requiring corrective action.

Suppose that a buyer has been buying galvanized pipe in standard lengths. The pipe is stored on racks in the storeroom. If the buyer should notice that a stockroom attendant almost always cuts the pipe to different lengths before issuing it, he ought to ask "why." His investigation might show that simply buying the pipe in random lengths would be justified— or, perhaps, that some of the pipe should be bought in exact cut-to-size lengths.

In other cases the buyer may find that so-called "convenience" packaging is actually a pain in the neck for shop employees. Examples: wire-nuts and other small fasteners mounted on cards or in blister-packs. Most workers would probably rather grab a handful of the parts out of a bulk packaging container.

Concerning use of purchased materials, the buyer should be alert for any situations where efficiency can be improved. This might be accomplished by providing workers with new materials or new tools. Different models of existing tools, or different types of existing materials, may also have to be considered.

The buyer should be especially aware of new maintenance problems that may arise when a manufacturing process is changed, or when a new piece of production equipment is installed. Whenever this happens, it will usually pay the buyer to get together with the maintenance crew, to re-think the whole question of MRO supplies and materials for the unit.

In addition, the buyer should always be on the lookout for cases where too much emphasis on standardization has shortchanged the man in the shop. Different sections of the plant often have completely different applications for supposedly "common" tools, and overly stringent standards may actually make things difficult for the man who has to use such tools.

If the buyer gets out into the shop often enough, he'll be able to correct such situations. And, to paraphrase the complaint that buyers often make about salesmen, he'll avoid any risk of the plant workers saying: "He placed the order and that was the last I saw of him."

25

THE BUYER AND QUALITY CONTROL

It's no accident that quality gets top billing in the "quality-service-price" phrase that most buyers use to describe the factors they consider in source selection. The single biggest responsibility a buyer has is to get acceptable goods into his plant.

Service and price are important too. Even the finest quality parts or materials lose a lot of their value if they don't arrive when production needs them. And, if he consistently pays premium prices for goods of any quality, the buyer will eventually undercut his firm's profit levels.

But, when you come right down to it, the buyer's primary concern must be with the quality of the goods he purchases. Poor quality materials or components not only disrupt manufacturing schedules from one end of the plant to the other—they often result in product failures and give the buyer's company a black eye throughout industry.

To guard against such situations, the buyer must know what quality is—and isn't. Quality is *not* an amorphous or indeterminate something that some vendors possess and others don't. Instead, it is a measurable and definable reflection of suppliers' ability to meet the buying company's specifications and tolerances.

In most companies, these specs and tolerances are established by engineering. On fabricated parts, they may involve dimensions, shapes, finishes and other factors. On raw materials, they may cover composition, tensile strength, hardness, brightness, machinability or corrosion-resistance.

But, no matter what type of specification is involved, it's a long, long road from the design engineer's concept to the receipt of workable goods at the front end of the buyer's production line. And, all along that road, good communications are a must.

Look at it this way. The buyer takes the specifications from engineering, and passes them along to the supplier's salesman. Then the supplier salesman transmits the specs to his production department; his quality control group (presumably) checks finished goods against the specs; and his shipping department sends OK'd items to the buyer's receiving/inspection dock.

Under such a set-up, which is a completely logical one, the buyer's quality control department becomes the final arbiter of how successfully each vendor maintains quality levels. And, as a direct result, the buyer must work hand-in-glove with quality control if he expects to do a good buying job.

At the very least, the buyer should get together with the QC manager, and work out a routine for recapping the quality performance of major vendors every quarter or so. (One way to do this might be to ask the QC manager for an extra copy of rejection reports, which could be filed in purchasing by supplier name. It would be especially helpful if the QC manager were to include pertinent handwritten comments on the file copy.)

Perhaps even more important, the really smart buyer will get to know his QC manager and the QC staff personally. He'll visit the quality control department frequently—not only to check specific orders, but to learn all he can about testing/inspection methods, equipment and techniques.

In some cases, the buyer's inquiries and questions will be technical in nature. He'll want to learn about ultrasonic inspection, X-ray techniques, and gauge calibration methods. He may even ask for a 10-minute personal lesson on how to use a micrometer or calipers.

In other cases, the buyer may want to cover some of the administrative angles of quality control work—such as statistical sampling methods and AQL's (acceptable quality levels). Here's a quick rundown on statistical sampling and AQL's:

ACCEPTABLE QUALITY LEVELS

QTY. RECD.	AQL 1.5 – TIGHTENED			AQL 2.5 – NORMAL		
	SAMPLE SIZE	ACCEPT	REJECT	SAMPLE SIZE	ACCEPT	REJECT
2-8	3	0	1	2	0	1
9-15	5	0	1	3	0	1
16-25	8	0	1	5	0	1
26-50	13	0	1	8	1	2
51-90	20	1	2	13	1	2
91-150	32	1	2	20	1	2
151-280	50	1	2	32	2	3
281-500	80	2	3	50	3	4
501-1200	125	3	4	80	5	6
1201-3200	200	5	6	125	7	8
3201-10000	315	8	9	200	10	11
10001-35000	500	12	13	315	14	15
35001-150000	800	18	19	500	21	22
150001-500000	1250	18	19	800	21	22
500001-OVER	2000	18	19	1250	21	22

Fig. 21 Because 100% inspection isn't practical on many items, statistical sampling programs are often used on incoming goods. Tables above highlight how quality standards (expressed as "acceptable quality levels") can be stiffened in either or both of two ways: increasing the size of the sample, or decreasing the number of allowable rejects in the sample.

The widespread use of statistical sampling is based on the fact that it is not economically practical, except on supercritical parts, to inspect every item in an incoming lot. Instead, the quality control manager sets up sampling methods based on statistical probabilities. Variable elements in these sampling methods include the size of the incoming lot, the size of the sample, and the number of rejects which the sample may contain without disqualifying the entire lot.

For different AQL's (the lower the AQL number, the more stringent the plan) there are different sampling criteria. And, according to the laws of probabilities, a sample lot's passing inspection means that the entire lot will probably fall within the buying company's quality tolerances. (There will be some rejects, but not enough to cause serious trouble.)

To see how this works, take a look at the two AQL tables in Fig. 21. They illustrate how a QC manager can stiffen his quality standards in either or both of two ways: by increasing the size of the lot sample, or by decreasing the number of allowable rejects in the sample.

Let's assume that the tables are being used in sampling inspection of two different parts—one with a tightened AQL of 1.5, the other with a normal AQL of 2.5.

If each incoming shipment contained 700 pieces, the randomly selected sample for the first part would be 125 pieces. And, if the sample contained 4 rejects, the entire lot of 700 would be rejected.

The sample for the second part would be only 80 pieces, however, and could contain 5 rejects without disqualifying the shipment.

The buyer's purpose, in learning all he can about his company's quality control procedures, is to gather pertinent information that he can then feed back to suppliers.

It's true that some firms prefer not to clue vendors in on the AQL's that they use—feeling that information of this kind may cause the suppliers to relax their quality standards. But, in any case, the buyer should inform his sources of the inspection methods and test apparatus that his company uses. (If they don't know the rules, how can suppliers play the game?)

Often—especially when new vendors or old vendors working on new parts are involved—the buyer may want to have the QC manager sit in on negotiating sessions. Such meetings are the perfect way to spell out all the conditions regarding pre-production samples, first-lot inspection criteria, etc.

The QC manager can also be of great help to the buyer in training and developing suppliers whose work is almost, but not quite, up to snuff. He can accompany the buyer on visits to suppliers' plants, can sit down with vendors' production and QC people, and can make all sorts of suggestions to turn marginal sources into acceptable ones.

For the buyer, this means an ever-broadening roster of sources that he can turn to. In addition, as they work closely with suppliers on quality control matters, the buyer and the QC manager may discover sources that are qualified for "certification" plans.

Under such plans, the buying company drills the selling company in the QC testing techniques that are needed for the item in question. Then the selling company takes over most of the QC details, subject only to spot checks on incoming material.

On many companies' organization charts, the phrase "quality control" has been replaced by "quality assurance." If the buyer works closely with his quality man by any name, he'll be assured of doing a better buying job.

PART FOUR

Supplier Relations

Of all the changes that the business world has seen in the last few years, one of the most far-reaching is the basic change in buyer/supplier relationships.

Where arm's-length relationships were once advocated as a matter of principle, if nothing else, more and more purchasing professionals are coming to recognize that good suppliers are key members of a buying company's team.

Their machinery and equipment are extensions of each customer's production facilities. Their imagination and creativity supplement the design skills of in-house engineers and outside R&D consultants. Their willingness to apply their specialized know-how can be one of the most positive forces in solving current problems facing any company.

You don't have to look far to find the reason why. With technology changing every day, it's increasingly difficult for any firm to have complete mastery of the state-of-the-art developments across industry. No firm is equipped or staffed for that kind of effort—not even conglomerates whose various divisions may span a broad number of engineering disciplines or production processes.

In most companies this means that major suppliers become the *de facto* experts on the goods and services required to manufacture an end product—with foundries providing help and guidance on casting specifications, steel mills counseling on metallurgical tolerances, and other suppliers furnishing similar data that is keyed to the items they sell.

A good vendor, in other words, knows his own product line to a fare-thee-well, whether it's a prime raw material or consumable supplies. And, to make maximum use of the supplier know-how that's available, a growing number of buyers are working more closely with their sources.

In some cases this closer cooperation means signing up for long-term contracts. In other cases it means inviting supplier salesmen and technical reps into the plant to look for trouble spots that may not even be apparent. In any case, the cooperative effort is one that simply won't work if the buyer adopts a paranoid "he must be out to get me some way" attitude.

None of this means that all vendor salesmen entering the buyer's office are the greatest guys who ever came down the pike. They're not. Some are outstanding, some are excellent, some are good, some are fair, and some are poor. Many will have ideas that the buyer can put to use— and more than a few will, in fact, be out to get the buyer if he's not careful.

As can be seen from the above, working with suppliers is one of the most demanding parts of a buyer's job because it involves a basic paradox. Ideally, in this area, the buyer has to be open-minded, warm-hearted, receptive to new ideas, skeptical, hard-nosed, inquisitive, demanding and persuasive—all at the same time.

To put it another way, perhaps a better analogy is this: the supplier is often like one of the family—but an in-law rather than a blood relation. The following chapters will discuss some of the specific problems that arise because of this unique relationship.

26

KEY QUESTIONS TO ASK ABOUT SUPPLIERS

Every newspaperman knows the key words that are critical in building a story: who, what, when, where, how and why. And, when it comes to knowing his suppliers better—getting a perspective of their strengths and weaknesses—buyers can put the same key words to good use.

The trick is simply to devise as many questions as possible around these words. The original questions will make you think of others. By the time you have answered them all, you'll have a good picture of the supplier and what he can do for your company.

Here are a few examples:

Who?—Who is the supplier? This looks straightforward enough, but it isn't always that simple. It often raises other questions such as: Who owns the firm? Is it a subsidiary of another organization? Is it a partnership or a corporation? Is it publicly traded? How is the stock traded: on a major exchange or over the counter?

Who represents the company locally: a dealer, distributor, or manufacturer's representative? Or, if the company is a dealer, what firms does it represent?

Who are the people in the supplier's firm? Who heads up sales? Production? Quality control? Shipping? Engineering?

And, for that matter, who are the supplier's other customers and what kind of business are they engaged in?

What?—What does the company supply? What are its major products? What items in the supplier's product line are applicable to your operations? What new items does the supplier have in the works?

What materials are required for the supplier's products? What are its sources? What kind of physical plant and equipment does the firm have? What unions are involved? What kind of labor relations history has it enjoyed?

When?—When do most orders arrive from the supplier: early, late, or on time? When did the salesman last call—and why? When will he probably call again—and why? When would be the best time to visit the supplier's plant? When should annual contract negotiations be reopened?

Where?—Where is the company located? Where are its central headquarters? Its sales offices? Plants? Service centers? Warehouses? Where should the buyer send his orders? Where should he direct requests for technical help? For maintenance service? For emergency expediting assistance?

Where (if applicable) are the points with which the supplier will offer freight equalization? Where are his sources of supply? Where in the buyer's plant are the areas that should be visited by the supplier's technical people?

How?—How much business does the buyer do with the supplier annually? How much of the buyer's requirements does this represent? How much of the supplier's total sales volume?

How does the supplier perform as a regular source of supply? How well does he meet quality/service/price requirements? How aware is he of the buyer's product line needs, buying procedures, and inspection techniques?

Why?—Why are you doing business with the supplier? Is it strictly a matter of price, quality or delivery—or a trade-off between all three? Is it a sole-source situation? Can you justify it if it is?

Why does the supplier want to do business with your firm? Are you just another customer to the head office; just another commission to the salesman? If so, why?

Why are the supplier's prices what they are? Are they established industry-wide? Could they be improved through negotiation or cost/price analysis? If not, why not?

This list isn't meant to be a complete rundown on all the questions you might want to ask yourself about a supplier. But, if you add those questions that are particularly pertinent to your company's operations or to its suppliers', you'll at least avoid taking your vendors for granted.

Obviously, no question should lend itself to a simple "yes" or "no" answer. For example, you many want a complete list of a supplier's production equipment, or a statistical summary on his performance for you.

But, starting with just six basic questions, you can make it a practice to develop a questioning attitude toward all your major suppliers. If you do, you'll inevitably wind up a better buyer.

27

VENDOR VISITS: THERE'S A LOT TO LOOK FOR

Every visit to a vendor's plant benefits the buyer in at least four ways. It will:

1. Help him get a better idea of the vendor's capabilities;

2. Keep him up to date on what's going on in the supplier's shop (including possible problems);

3. Give him a practical insight into manufacturing techniques, including new ones that may be developing;

4. Forge stronger lines of communication between the buyer and the vendor's staff.

As a result, smart buyers make the most of every visit—using these four points as a sort of checklist. No matter what the primary purpose of a field trip may be, they look for advantages in the other areas as well.

There are, after all, many reasons why a buyer visits a vendor's plant. He may be invited as part of an open-house for customers. The occasion may be the dedication of a new facility being opened by a supplier. On the other hand, the buyer may be visiting the plant as a member of a formal source-inspection team. Or, he may have made the trip to raise hell about delinquent orders or poor quality.

The wise buyer makes full use of every opportunity offered by such vendor visits. He doesn't restrict himself to narrow discussions or observations, but uses a broad-scope approach in digging out information.

In practical terms, this means that the buyer who has made a visit to check deliveries with the front office will also take time to tour the plant. And one who is primarily interested in checking facilities will also check the delivery status of all open orders before he leaves.

Here's a list of the areas in a vendor's plant which a visiting buyer should look at:

The front office: Don't hesitate to get to know the supplier's top management; it can pay off in many ways. At the very least, ask to see the top man in sales, and, ideally, also get together with the company president.

Such interviews serve a double purpose. On the one hand, you can use them to size up the supplier's top brass. You can get an idea not only of their technical experience and background, but also of their attitude. And management attitude, according to some of the most skilled vendor evaluators in the purchasing profession, is one of the surest indicators of a supplier's probable performance.

On the other hand, you can use interviews with vendor management to emphasize the needs and buying policies of your firm.

In such interviews, don't be afraid to ask probing, even embarrassing questions. ("How come your number three machine is down?" "Why all the congestion in the shipping room?" "Are you the guy my expediter should call if he really wants some action?") Such questions will demonstrate that you're not there for idle chit-chat—which is precisely the point you want to make.

The shop: In the shop, you'll want to look over machinery and equipment, assessing age, type and operating condition. You'll also want to observe general housekeeping practices, to see if the plant is neat, clean and safe.

With luck, the vendor may be running one of your jobs when you tour the shop. If so, be sure to stop and speak to the men actually working on the machines. Identify yourself as the customer. Compliment them on their performance if this is warranted, but don't fake such compliments. Your aim, basically, is to convert your company from a faceless customer into something represented by a live, flesh-and-blood person.

Engineering and R&D: If you stop by engineering and research, you may get an insight into some of the vendor's state-of-the-art developments. At the very least, you can spot how many people are engaged in these activities. This will help you gauge the firm's commitment to look-ahead projects.

The purchasing department: By all means visit the purchasing department. Quiz the purchasing agent about his policies and systems. If he has a purchasing manual, ask him for a copy (even if only on a loan basis). The same goes for copies of welcome booklets, purchasing newsletters, or any other printed material he has available.

By taking such literature back to your own plant, you can read it at your leisure. It will give you a pretty good idea of how effective the vendor's purchasing set-up is. And, while you're there in person, be sure to zero in on really critical factors.

For example, you'll want the P.A. to spell out precisely how he feels about sole-sourcing. (If a strike should hit one of his major suppliers, and he didn't have an alternate, it could jeopardize his deliveries to you.)

Also, you should ask him to describe his general methods for selecting and evaluating vendors, with particular emphasis on how quality and reliability are rated.

Production control: In this area, you should be on the alert to see how effective the vendor's scheduling systems are. A visit here should also determine how closely material schedulers work with purchasing. You might want to ask how internal lead times are developed—and see if the answers jibe with purchasing's comments on the matter.

Inventory control: Here again, you should check out coordination with purchasing. In addition, find out the inventory policy on purchased goods. Too rapid a turnover (unless supported by a stockless purchasing or systems contracting plan) might increase the danger of stockouts and work stoppages. Too slow a turnover, conversely, might mean that the company has too much capital tied up in stock.

Take a look also at how inventory is stored, and don't confine this scrutiny to any one class of materials. You should inspect stocks of all kinds: raw materials and other purchased goods, work-in-process, and finished goods inventory.

Quality control: An in-person visit to the quality control area should fill you in on inspection techniques, gauge calibration methods, etc. And, in looking over all aspects of the QC department, you should

VENDOR SURVEY

Name of Company (Including Corporate Organizations, Divisions or Other Affiliations)

_____

_____

PLANT SURVEY

Company Operates   Address of Plant Surveyed _____
   Single Plant ( )   _____
   Multiple Plant ( )   _____

Net Worth _____

Annual Sales Volume (Total Company) _____   Telephone No. _____

Plant   Personnel

No. Sq. Ft. _____   No. Employees _____
Condition _____   Unions _____
Type of Construction _____
_____

Ownership - Corporation ( ) Partnership ( ) Private ( )

Financial - D & B attached ( )

Present Company Officials: Company Security Clearance _____

1. _____   _____
2. _____
3. _____

Facilities - List Attached ( )
(Include Mfg. and Quality Control Facilities)

End Products: _____
_____

References - (Customers)

1. _____
2. _____
3. _____

DO NOT WRITE BELOW THIS LINE ═══════════════════════════════

Recommended For: _____
_____
_____

General Information: _____
_____
_____

QUALITY CONTROL APPROVAL	MFG. ENGINEERING APPROVAL	TREASURY DEPT. APPROVAL	PURCHASING APPROVAL
Date	Date	Date	Date

Fig. 22 Survey sheets like this one can be filled out during and after visits to suppliers' plants, as a permanent record of key information gathered.

again take a broad view. Quality techniques on both incoming and out-going materials should be closely examined.

In addition, you should check out the paperwork systems involved. If there's a QC manual or other write-up available, ask for a copy to take back with you.

The shipping dock: Here's your chance to see how effective the vendor is in scheduling and routing inbound and outbound materials. Typical danger signals: lines of trucks backed up, with drivers fuming; piles of material, received but not logged in; inadequate packaging; etc.

In addition, this is your chance to get on a first-name basis with the supplier's shipping clerk—who often has make-or-break power over rush deliveries that you may need.

Don't forget, though, that you can also offer help to the various groups that you visit in a vendor's plant. Perhaps you can assist the P.A. with an expediting problem, where you're a big customer of one of his suppliers. Or you may be able to give him tips on shortcut buying systems that you've developed in your own plant, or give him ideas on possible new sources.

In the final analysis, a successful plant visit depends on the buyer's seeing everyone and everything he should, asking pertinent questions, and providing the information a supplier justifiably requires.

To make a record of vendor visits, many firms use survey sheets such as that illustrated in Fig. 22. Such sheets can readily be filled out and made part of a supplier record system. But, whether you use record sheets or not, visits to vendors' plants should open up new vistas of information for you.

28

HOW TO HANDLE PROBLEM SALESMEN

Dealing with salesmen is one of a buyer's main duties, and good salesmen can make a buyer look good. They can feed him all sorts of new ideas and market data, and help him serve as an information clearinghouse for all operating departments.

Unfortunately, however, not all salesmen are good salesmen. Here's a list of some of the less-than-ideal types—together with suggestions on how to handle them:

The wind-bag: This salesman could also be dubbed the back-slapper, the joke-teller or the time-waster. He often drops in just because he "happens to be in the neighborhood."

In short, he's a socializer—only too happy to tell you about his grandchildren or golf game, but often reluctant to talk business or stick to the point.

Two time-tested techniques are still best for getting the wind-bag out of your office so you can return to work. One is simply to stand up,

stick out your hand (which he'll have to grasp) and then steer him to
the door.

The other method is to have your secretary buzz you on the phone
after the interview has gone on for 15 minutes or so. You can then logically tell the salesman that an emergency has come up, and that he'll
have to excuse you.

The technocrat: This salesman probably thinks of himself as a
"marketing engineer." And, whether or not he has a technical degree,
he'll try to snow you with engineeringese. He may even have his memo
pads printed on graph paper, and will probably lard his conversation
with references such as "incremental magnitudes" and "frammis tolerances."

What he may be trying to do, in fact, is overawe you with (a) the
complexity of his product line, and (b) his own technical competence.
If he's successful, the logical outcome is (c): your sending him on to see
the design or production engineers. If this happens, you'll simply be ad-
mitting that you're incapable of talking business with this salesman.

Of course there will be cases where you will want to refer a salesman to engineering or production. But especially on initial sales calls,
there are very practical ways to meet the technocrat's gambits.

The best method is to emphasize that—no matter how complex or
highly engineered his product line is—there is basic information about his
firm that he must supply to purchasing.

Ask him for a facilities list, a roster of other companies presently
buying from his company, credit references, and for specific percentages
on his firm's quality/delivery performance for its present customers.

If he doesn't have the material in his briefcase, suggest that he mail
it in to you so you and the engineers can discuss it in detail together before his next call.

The name-dropper: "Your Mr. Zilch suggested that I drop in to
see you," is a typical name-dropper's opening. And, if Mr. Zilch is the
company president, the buyer is bound to wonder what it's all about.

When this happens, the buyer's best technique is to be completely
straightforward. He should tell the salesman that he'll be happy to hear
his presentation, and should then follow the normal routine for any sales
call. At the conclusion of the interview, however, the buyer should tell
the salesman that he will review the discussion with the executive who
made the referral.

Above all, the buyer shouldn't be pressured into giving orders or promises of orders. It's quite possible that the name-dropper has simply taken the executive's name from a copy of the annual report—and doesn't know him from Adam.

The silent type: Just as frustrating as the salesmen you can't turn off are the ones you can't turn on. Whether inarticulate or simply bashful, they come in, shake hands, and then just sit.

In handling the silent type (and remember, it might be his firm that has a new product you could use), you've got to assume that he does know what he's selling.

So, ask him what his product line is. Then, if your company does have an application for the item, tell the salesman how you use it. Stress to him that you are looking for new ideas and helpful suggestions. Outline any current problems that need solutions, and emphasize that your firm looks for supplier help in these areas.

By laying it on the line in this way, you may jolt him into some sort of reaction.

The newsboy: This salesman typically arrives with an attaché case containing two or three 1,000-page catalogs—plus an assortment of price lists, sales brochures, illustrated fliers, die-cut pamphlets, etc.

Then he wants to stand behind you and go through each piece page by page—perhaps reading selected passages aloud.

The best way to handle the newsboy is to point out that group reading may be sociable—but it's an awful waste of his time and yours. Suggest that he leave behind any particularly pertinent literature (90% of it is probably designed as leave-behind material, anyway) so you can give it the time it deserves.

If you want to, give him five minutes to red-circle any pamphlet sections that he wants to call to your specific attention. Or let him put paper clips on catalog pages that he considers must-reading for you.

The know-nothing: When a salesman arrives inadequately prepared on your company and its line of business, it's sometimes because he hasn't been briefed sufficiently by his superiors. This often happens when the salesman is new.

The most gracious way to handle this situation is to be frank about it. Tell the salesman that you have already gone over your firm's buying policies and systems with his predecessor or sales manager. Suggest that he return to see you after he's had a rebriefing with his company's sales executives.

The order-taker: Unlike the know-nothing, the order-taker may
be completely familiar with your company's needs and with how his firm
fits into them. The trouble with this type of salesman, though, is that he's
weak on follow-through. While he's only too happy to write up orders
for your new needs, he can't fill you in on the status of the orders you
gave him last week or a month ago.

This means that he may have to call his office before he can give
you any meaningful information on what's happening back at his shop.
For handling an order-taker, a hard-nosed approach is best. Tell him that
there won't be any new orders until he briefs you on the current ones.

If he has to call his office to get the data, don't let him make the
call from your desk. Insist that he trek back out to a pay phone in your
lobby or reception room, and then tell the receptionist when he is ready
to talk.

Mr. Peepers: This salesman probably learned to read upside down
before he mastered the right-side-up method—and he puts his special skill
to use by reading everything on your desk.

One way to forestall the Mr. Peepers is to clear your desk prior to
all interviews. This isn't too practical, however, when you're simultaneously working on several projects and have salesmen dropping in throughout the day.

A very effective alternative is simply to keep a large, outdated blue-
print—or organizational chart—beside your desk at all times. Then,
when a salesman is on his way in to see you, you can unfold the print
or chart and spread it over everything on your desk. And if you want to
teach a Mr. Peepers some manners, you can wait until he starts his eye-
balling before you ostentatiously unfold the sheet and spread it out.

In the long term, of course, you've got to educate your salesmen.
You've got to turn poor ones into good ones. But the techniques listed
above should give you a little more time for interviewing sales reps who
are already good salesmen.

29

25 STEPS TO BETTER SUPPLIER RELATIONS

Smart buyers know that their success in purchasing, and their professional progress, depend largely on suppliers.

A good supplier can bail a buyer out on delivery problems, feed him all sorts of cost-saving ideas, and make him look like a hero instead of a has-been or never-was.

All this means that "good supplier relations" isn't an empty phrase to be given lip-service in manuals or reports, but never put into practice day by day at the buyer's desk. Quite the contrary, it's a goal that every buyer should actively pursue every minute of his working day.

Since most of a buyer's contact with a supplier firm is through the salesman on the account, it's in dealing with salesmen that he has the most frequent opportunities to build mutual good will. And since salesmen are people, the buyer's dealings with them should be characterized by plenty of tact, diplomacy, and common decency or good manners.

Here's a list of 25 pointers to follow in dealing with salesmen:

1. *Do* see visiting salesmen promptly, so they don't waste time cooling their heels in the reception room. Time is just as valuable to them as it is to you, and they're often severely limited as to the number of calls they can make in a working day.

2. *Don't* let phone calls or a stream of unannounced visitors from other departments interrupt the interview. In some cases such interruptions may be unavoidable, but try to have your secretary screen all but top-priority calls and visitors.

3. *Do* advise unsuccessful bidders of the disposition of their quotes. Tell them why they didn't get the order: high price, inability to meet specs or delivery, etc. Don't keep them in the dark, trying to guess what you've decided on their bid.

4. *Don't* be over-jealous of your buying prerogatives. Don't try to bluff your way if you don't understand the technicalities of the salesman's product line. Give him a chance, in a joint meeting, to state his case to your technical people.

5. *Do* respect any confidential data that the salesman divulges to you. Make sure everyone in your company understands that this is the purchasing department's policy—to be followed across the board.

6. *Don't* play favorites based on personalities or anything other than past quality/service performance. If one supplier is allowed to re-bid, for example, all competing bidders should also be given another crack at the business.

7. *Don't* ask for rush deliveries unless you absolutely have to. Check using departments' "emergency" requests to make sure that the crisis is real, not imaginary. Too often, shipments that a salesman has gone all out for sit on the receiving dock for days.

8. *Do* introduce the salesman to your boss and to anyone who may have to fill in for you during your absence. Let the salesman know that you and your associates realize he's a flesh-and-blood individual, not just a faceless name.

9. *Don't* go over the salesman's head—in negotiating, expediting, or any business matter, unless you have to. And if you have to work something out directly with a sales manager or other top brass in a supplier firm, keep the salesman posted.

10. *Don't* be too hesitant about letting the salesman use your name or your company's in testimonials. Unless proprietary data is involved, you shouldn't object to his advertising the fact that he's done a good job for you and your firm.

11. *Do* suggest other firms that you think might be able to use his

products or services. Sales leads are a vital part of a salesman's livelihood; he'll be especially grateful for any realistic ones that you can give him.

12. *Don't,* except under extreme circumstances, threaten to blacklist him with your friends and acquaintances in the purchasing profession. (If you do make such threats, be prepared to carry them out.)

13. *Do* keep him posted on what you think of his performance, and of the performance of his firm. If you have a formal vendor rating system, schedule regular sessions where you can discuss his "grades" with him, and can suggest ways to improve them.

14. *Do* offer to help his purchasing department in any way you can: suggesting systems improvements; expediting the supplier's orders with firms where you swing a lot of weight; providing copies of your own policies and procedures manual, etc.

15. *Do* explain your own paperwork systems in detail. Spell out buying methods, receiving procedures, and all the other administrative techniques with which the supplier's systems must mesh for maximum efficiency.

16. *Do* visit the supplier's plant or warehouse—and make it a working trip rather than a junket. Take notes and write up a formal report. Let the salesman check the accuracy of the factual data that you assemble during the visit.

17. *Don't* keep him in the dark regarding your company's current product line, or on new items you may be planning to market unless these are still confidential. Give him a chance to assist in product design before designs are frozen.

18. *Do* take him on a tour of your plant, giving him a first-hand chance to see how his products are used and spot any situations where he might be able to suggest alternate manufacturing methods in the goods he produces, etc.

19. *Do* explain your quality/inspection methods: acceptable quality level formulas, statistical sampling techniques, off-site certification standards that are acceptable, etc. He can't shoot for top-quality performance unless you give him these guidelines to take back to his plant.

20. *Do* share the expenses for the business luncheons that you have with him; alternate in picking up the checks. Or, if your firm has a company cafeteria or lunchroom, invite him in if his visit takes place around the noon hour.

21. *Don't* look for entertainment or gifts of any kind from him— or ask him for any special deals on personal purchases for yourself or

any other company employee. If possible, try to get this prohibition expressed in writing as a matter of policy by the head of purchasing, with an endorsement by the chief executive officer.

22. *Don't* complain if you can't get the salesman on the phone in the middle of the day. Selling is his business. You can't expect him to remain desk-bound waiting for calls from customers; he has to be out on the street finding new customers and new orders.

23. *Do* let him know that you expect local calls to be answered by the end of the day. He should have some method for keeping in touch with his office, and for having calls such as yours relayed to him promptly.

24. *Do* explain your company's policies on choosing suppliers, and on all the questions that invariably crop up whenever two firms are engaged in buying and selling. Typical examples: what's the policy on overruns and under-runs, what's the starting point for computation of cash discount time periods, etc.

25. *Don't* let the salesman's natural eagerness for more and more orders get him into a situation where your business accounts for practically all of his plant's capacity. Such situations can spell trouble in the long run. Encourage the salesman to get new accounts so neither he nor his firm will be completely dependent on your company's business.

30

DON'T GET CAUGHT IN THE SAMPLE–TRAMPLE

A tricky problem plaguing most buyers is what to do about (and with) vendors' samples. Just about all salesmen are eager to furnish buyers with samples if the nature of their product line permits. They figure that by doing this they may get an order. At worst, they get an opportunity to call on the buyer again—either to pick the sample up, to get a report on its performance, or both.

However, for buyers, the salesman's readiness to provide samples of his goods can pose all sorts of administrative, ethical and legal problems. Here are some typical questions that arise as soon as a buyer has accepted a sample:

Who pays for the sample? If it's free, is it furnished completely without obligation, or only for a specific test period? If it's to be paid for, what account should be charged? Who should make out the requisition? And, whether the sample is on a free or paid-for basis, who's to pay for running tests on it?

Complicating the whole issue is the fact that many samples arrive by mail or other delivery channels, completely "unsolicited" as far as the buyer is concerned. Later, it may turn out that engineers or other shop personnel have requested the samples. They often do this by clipping coupons in magazines, or filling out sample-request forms at trade shows. But for purchasing and receiving the result is the same: a long row of shelves littered with vials and mini-packages, awaiting disposition when someone gets around to it.

The best bet for resolving the problems that arise with vendors' samples is to set up a firm policy regarding such trial lots. This policy should state that a sample will be accepted only when there is a definite possibility that the buying company may benefit from its inspection or test.

A buyer should not accept a sample at all unless it means potentially lower prices, better quality, or the possibility of qualifying a supplier whose addition to the approved-source list would in itself be desirable.

This statement should be in writing—perhaps as part of purchasing's policy manual—and should be called to the attention of engineers and other operating personnel. In addition, it should state that all samples are to be paid for by the buying company.

To understand the reasons for this, consider the hazards of alternative courses. Although it may seem fair for a company to accept samples free of charge, and then assume the testing costs itself, such a set-up doesn't really split the financial burden. Often the costs of tests will outweigh the cost of the sample. Or, in some cases, the reverse may be true.

The big objection to accepting free samples, however, is that this puts the buyer under an obligation. Having given something away for nothing, the supplier can justifiably claim that the product should be tested. He may want to be present at the tests—and he'll certainly say that he's entitled to a report on the test results.

For the buyer, this can lead to all sorts of problems: setting up testing timetables, arranging meetings, negotiating testing methods, etc.

Paying for all vendors' samples, in contrast, simplifies everything for the buyer. He can test or not test, as he wishes. If he does decide to test, he can do it when he wants to. He can use his own test standards, and he is not obligated to tell the vendor either the results or the testing methods used.

The vendor, similarly, is protected because few buyers will pay for samples unless they're serious about testing them and considering the supplier as a potential source. Even if the vendor isn't completely satisfied under such a set-up, at least he hasn't incurred any out-of-pocket expenses.

None of this means that the buyer should be unnecessarily hard-nosed about accepting legitimate samples. Smart buyers, however, will be judicious in accepting samples—and will always insist on paying for those that they do accept. In doing so, they'll avoid many problems that might otherwise arise.

31

WHEN YOU CAN'T SEE WHAT YOU'RE BUYING

Every company, at least now and then, has to buy intangible services. It may want to call in a management consultant to review systems and procedures. Perhaps it has a product or package design job that it wants to farm out to specialists. Or the sales department may want to contract for a market study by some outside research group.

When this happens, the buyer may get a requisition reading something like this:

"To cover the XYZ Co.'s fees for services, as discussed with Mr. Jones." And Mr. Jones, of course, is the requisitioner or department head who is authorizing the contract for services.

One way to handle such requisitions is to let them go through unedited, and have the order typist transcribe them verbatim. This is an easy way out, and the buyer can justify his action (or lack of it) by telling himself that "there really wasn't anything he could add to the transaction, anyway."

The trouble with this approach is that the buyer using it is shirking his responsibility. It's his job to monitor the commercial aspects of all his company's contracts—and this means agreements for intangible services as much as it does p.o.'s for a gross of bolts or a piece of capital equipment.

Usually, to get the data needed for writing a tight contract, the buyer will have to go back to the requisitioner. He'll also have to call the vendor in, for negotiation of the contract's fine points. And often, in both cases, he may meet with resistance.

The requisitioner may feel that the buyer is trying to monkey with the technical content and scope of the agreement. And the supplier of the service—especially if his calling card says he's a "creative designer" —may think himself above such mundane matters as discussion of terms and conditions.

(Typical comment: "Why, we hardly ever work against purchase orders . . .")

In either case, there's an easy way to meet such opposition. Point out to the requisitioner that your concern is solely with the contract's commercial aspects. Remind him that a good contract will prevent him from being burned by poor supplier performance or overcharges. And, as far as the supplier is concerned, you have an extremely potent bargaining point. Explain that your company expects all suppliers to work against formal contracts—and that that is why you received a requisition for his services in the first place.

The first time you have to write a contract for intangible services, it may be difficult. You may not know where to start. But once you get the hang of it, it won't be that bothersome. Here are a few suggestions:

As a general rule (unless your firm has a special form for such contracts), you should write the agreement on a standard purchase order form. Handling it in this way, you get the benefit of the standard terms and conditions on your p.o. form—plus whatever special terms you put in the text of the contract.

For ready reference (and to insure that you cover all important points), you may want to set the contract up with three main subject areas: "Scope of the work," "Price," and "Performance scheduling."

In effect, these subjects correspond to the three points that must be nailed down on any purchase order: item description and specifications; unit or lot price; and delivery date. If you keep this in mind, it may help you in phrasing the contract.

Take "scope of the work," for example. The thing to do in this area is to go to the requisitioner, and ask him to tell you—in three or four sentences—just what he expects the consultant to do.

If you take notes during this discussion, and ask questions about any points that don't seem clear, you should be able to draft a fairly concise statement of what the consultant is supposed to do for your firm. Perhaps you can't be 100% specific in this statement of the contract's scope—but be as specific as you can.

Suppose that your accounting department wants a management consultant to study its accounts receivable routines. For such a service, your contract's scope-of-work section might read like this:

"Seller hereby contracts to review the buyer's systems now in use for processing customer orders, and to provide specific recommendations for improving the systems. Such recommendations shall include, but not be limited to, methods for improving buyer's control of customer orders, for shortening order-processing time, and for reducing clerical effort."

This part of the contract should also name the individual in the buyer's company (the accounting manager, in this case) who will judge whether and when the vendor has satisfactorily completed contract performance. In addition, it should specify what if any tangible items are to be delivered as part of contract performance.

For a management consultant's services, these tangible items might be flow-charts or systems write-ups on new methods. For a creative designer they might be artwork renditions, hand-made product or package samples, blueprints or drawings, bills of material for eventual production in volume, etc.

Setting up the "price" section of an intangible-services contract isn't very difficult, either—even though you may have to include data on how the fee is to be calculated and when it's to be paid.

The easiest way of handling the price, of course, is to establish a fixed fee to be paid on satisfactory completion of the services. But, even if you have to work out a schedule for compensation—based on the consultant's man-hours—there are certain safeguards you can set up.

The first of these is to spell out the names of the consultant's personnel who will be working on your project. You should also specify the daily or hourly rates for each of these men, since a senior staffer's time is worth more than a junior's. You should also establish a flat rate for the supplier's clerical support services.

Then, with this information on the contract, you can request an itemized statement on each invoice for consultants' time—and the statement will mean something to you.

Equally important, the contract should also specify what justifiable "expenses" are—whether for travel or supplies—and should establish standard rates for these expenses.

Since many consultants want to submit invoices during the course of their work, you should have some financial method for keeping them motivated until contract completion. One of the best ways is to withhold payment on a small part of each bill—perhaps 10%—until the final work has been completed to the requisitioner's satisfaction.

Since any consultant-type activity falls naturally into a logical series of steps, you should specify these steps in the contract covering the service. Doing this will take care of the "performance scheduling" part of the agreement.

Here again, you'll probably have to ask the requisitioner's guidance in determining the major milestones of the task to be done. But, once you have them outlined and stated in the contract, you should also ask the supplier for regular reports during the course of the work.

In a way, these reports will be continuing "acknowledgments," and perhaps you can tie the scheduling of the reports in with the supplier's submission of invoices. Under such a system, the consultant would have to furnish progress and forecast reports with each bill, in order to get payment.

In many cases you'll want to cover other areas in your contracts. If a consultant is doing design work for you, you should definitely have a tight "save harmless" clause on patent infringement. It's also good to notify such suppliers that drawings and prints are confidential material, and must be handled as such. Or, if some consultants are going to do on-site work in hazardous areas of your plant, an insurance clause is a must.

All told, setting up intangible service contracts isn't that tough. Ask a lot of questions and nail down all the specifics that you can, and you'll certainly wind up with a better contract than if you didn't query the requisition at all.

32

EXPEDITING IS THE BUYER'S JOB, TOO

Whether it's called "expediting" or "follow-up," one of the most important parts of a buyer's job is getting goods into the plant or office when they're needed. This is just as true when the buyer has a full-time expediting staff at his disposal as it is when he handles follow-up duties as part of his formal job description.

The reason is that the buyer has the negotiating muscle when it comes to getting suppliers to live up to their delivery promises, or, in some cases, to better them. He is the one who makes the decisions on how future business will be awarded, so he naturally becomes the one to whom suppliers will listen most intently when current delivery problems are being discussed.

Today, with more and more companies striving to keep inventories at rock-bottom levels to conserve operating capital, good expediting techniques are more important than ever. If something goes wrong, a line may be shut down or other production difficulties may result. Let's take a look then at several areas where the buyer has a big stake in expediting methods.

The first area concerns the mechanics and systems of expediting. Whether a separate expediter or the buyer himself handles the follow-up work, there must be an established routine to keep open orders from being lost in the shuffle of other duties.

The best way to implement such a system is to set up a tickler or follow-up file in which open orders are identified by date. This date should be the day on which some sort of review should be made, to determine if the goods will be shipped on time, or have been shipped on time.

Many companies like to use a special card-stock or tag-stock copy of the purchase order for this kind of file. This makes it easy to file the copies vertically in an open-top tub file, and to use colored tabs or signals as markers along the visible edge.

No matter what type of system a company uses, however, there should also be some method for grouping open orders by supplier as well as by due date. This enables the expediter or buyer to get a complete rundown on all open orders when he's on the phone getting information. In companies where a computer kicks out expediting printouts, this is no problem. In firms relying on manual methods, the buyer may want to help the expediter set up a cross index file to accomplish this.

To get expediting information from suppliers, whoever does follow-up can use telephone calls, wires, letters, forms or postcards. (On long-distance phone calls, a good rule is this: reverse the charges when the call is being made because of the supplier's delinquency; pick up the tolls yourself when the call is required because of internal problems such as production scheduling foul-ups.)

One method that many companies use is to have their p.o. forms printed with extra "tracer" copies built into the basic set. Then, when follow-up is required, it's easy to extract the tracer copy and shoot it off to the vendor.

Fig. 23 illustrates the tracer copy that Champion Dish Washing Machine Co. uses for this kind of follow-up. Note how the upper right corner of this tracer copy is used to get a basic motivational message across:

"All orders are rated on meeting delivery requirements. Our purchase orders are placed based on a vendor's performance."

(This is something any buyer could rubber-stamp on existing tracer copies, if he wanted to.)

Other firms prefer to use standard or custom-printed follow-up

ITEM NO.	PART #	QTY.	MATERIAL DESCRIPTION	UNIT	UNIT PRICE	

PURCHASE ORDER NO. C

NOTE

ALL ORDERS ARE RATED ON MEETING DELIVERY REQUIREMENTS. OUR PURCHASE ORDERS ARE PLACED BASED ON A VENDOR'S PERFORMANCE.

PURCHASE ORDER FOLLOW-UP

PLEASE DIRECT AN **IMMEDIATE REPLY** ON THE ITEMS CHECKED BELOW
TO CHAMPION - P. O. BOX 4149 NORTH STATION - WINSTON-SALEM, N. C. 27105

☐ Please mail your acknowledgment copy of this order.

☐ When will you ship the balance of this order?

☐ Why didn't you ship as promised? Advise shipping date.

☐ It is imperative that you ship the above order to arrive by no later than _____

PURCHASE ORDER – FOLLOW UP.

Fig. 23 Tracer copy of Champion Dish Washing Machine Co.'s purchase order set is typical of follow-up copies provided at the time original order is typed. Note message in upper right corner of this copy, which reminds suppliers that on-time delivery is one of the factors considered in awarding future orders.

WRIGHT LINE
Div. of BARRY WRIGHT CORP.
Worcester 6, Mass.

DATE _____

PLEASE FURNISH THE FOLLOWING INFORMA-
TION REGARDING OUR ORDER NO. _____

DATED _____ YOUR NO. _____

1. ☐ WILL/DID YOU SHIP ON_____AS REQUESTED?

2. ☐ WILL/DID YOU SHIP ON_____AS PROMISED?

3. ☐ MATERIAL URGENTLY NEEDED, GIVE BEST
   POSSIBLE SHIPPING DATE.

4. ☐ WHEN WILL YOU SHIP BALANCE DUE?

5. ☐ CAN YOU SHIP PARTIAL AT ONCE?

6. ☐ THIS IS SECOND REQUEST FOR
   INFORMATION.
   YOUR CO-OPERATION IS REQUESTED.

7. ☐ ACKNOWLEDGEMENT, STATING PRICE
   AND DELIVERY.

8. ☐ _____
   _____
   _____

*Please answer promptly, on the
attached card.*

THANK YOU

BY _____
                    PURCHASING DEPT.

DATE _____

GENTLEMEN:

REFERRING TO YOUR ORDER NO. _____

OUR NO. _____

☐ 1. WE WILL/DID SHIP ON_____AS REQUESTED.

☐ 2. WE WILL/DID SHIP ON_____AS PROMISED.

☐ 3. OUR BEST SHIPPING DATE IS _____.

☐ 4. BALANCE WILL BE SHIPPED _____.

☐ 5. WILL SHIP PARTIAL QTY. OF _____
     AT ONCE.

☐ 6. SECOND REQUEST ACKNOWLEDGED.

☐ 7. PRICE AND DELIVERY DATA BEING
     FORWARDED.

☐ 8. _____
     _____
     _____

BY _____ TITLE _____

FIRM _____

ADDRESS _____

CITY & STATE _____

Fig. 24 Double-size postcards, like this one used by the Wright Line, can readily be adapted to follow-up uses. Card folds over so supplier's name and address are visible when the card is originally mailed; portion with supplier's comments is backed up with postpaid mailing indicia and Wright Line's name/address.

forms (many of which are multi-ply sets with a copy that the vendor can use for his reply). Expediting postcards are also popular.

Fig. 24 shows the text that the Wright Line uses on its double-size expediting postcard. The illustration on the left is the company's request for information; the illustration on the right is the area where the supplier makes his reply. When the card is folded over for mailing, the vendor's name and address appears on the addressee side; when it's torn apart for mailing back, the Wright Line's name and address is on the reverse.

With systems aids like these, getting information to and from suppliers isn't much of a problem. But the second duty of expediting that's of vital concern to every buyer is in the area of buyer/expediter cooperation.

First, you have to develop standard terminology for the comments that you and the expediter may jot down on follow-up copies. If each of you develops his own unique brand of shorthand and abbreviations, chances are the other one won't be able to decipher such notes. Establish a few standard terms and phrases for common notes such as "Will ship," "Pro number," "Trailer Number," "Car Number," "Flight Number," etc. Then there won't be any misinterpretations when you refer to the expediter's comments, or he refers to yours. (The same advantage holds true when you do your own expediting; your comments will be understandable to any other buyer who has to refer to your open order file, as his will be to you.)

Second, and even more important, you have to ask your expediter for regular rundowns on various suppliers' reliability—*and you have to listen to him*. Don't brush him off when he complains that some suppliers are chronic offenders in maintaining good delivery performance. He's not trying to make his own job easier (although this may be a secondary effect)—he's trying to give you the inputs that you need for your decision-making as a buyer.

Third, you've got to back your expediter up when need be—perhaps by making follow-up calls from your own desk. Often, you may make such calls to a higher level in the supplier's firm—and the very fact that you are making the call gives it more impact and leverage.

As noted earlier, your position as the buyer gives you this bargaining clout. But you should also make every effort to impress suppliers with a basic message: "When the expediter speaks, he speaks for me."

One way to get this message across is to arrange for the expediter to sit in with you, from time to time, on supplier interviews. Have him lay it on the line to salesmen whose firms aren't living up to their delivery promises. Encourage him to give specific examples: order numbers, days late, the impact on your firm, etc. Then, when he's finished, tell the salesman something like this:

"Okay, you've heard the facts. Now tell *us* what you're going to do about it."

In some cases you may have to award orders to firms whose delivery performance isn't what it should be—perhaps because proprietary items or special tooling is involved. In such cases, your expediter may wind up tearing his hair out by the roots in his efforts to get the goods in on time. But—and this is the fourth and final point on buyer/expediter cooperation—you can at least explain the situation to the expediter when you're forced into such a position. If you do this, he won't think you're a stubborn so-and-so who never listens to him. And, when you give him the background, you can also warn him that the upcoming order may involve delivery problems and that he should stay right on top of it from the day it's placed.

Another area of expediting that concerns the buyer is what might be called preventive expediting. This simply means that you select reliable sources to begin with—making sure that their production and distribution facilities fit the specific needs you ask them to handle. As noted just above, you may not always be able to do this—but at least you should make every effort to do so.

Another part of preventive expediting is making sure that every supplier understands your delivery needs. Work with salesmen on this, and on anyone else in the supplier firm who has a say in scheduling customers' orders. Keep hammering home the message that delivery promises on an order are just as inviolable as price or specifications of the item being ordered.

Also, as part of preventive expediting, explore your company's internal systems to discover the reasons why supposedly normal and routine orders suddenly turn into crisis-situations. Look into production scheduling and inventory control methods, and make sure that everybody in the company knows applicable lead times. The fewer times you have to call on suppliers for expediting assistance required by your company's miscalculations, the better service you'll get in such cases. You will also strengthen your position for demanding top-notch delivery performance in general from suppliers.

Because expediting is fundamentally a problem-solving function (the word itself comes from the Latin for "to free one caught by the foot") there will always be situations where corrective action is needed on a rush basis.

When this happens, the best bet is to pool all the resources available to both the buying and selling companies, to resolve the situation.

If the supplier is in a bind, for example, try to isolate the various problems he's having. Is he short of material? Does he have a machine down for lack of a spare part? In either of these cases, you may be able to help with your own purchasing know-how and support. Perhaps you can expedite his orders for materials or components, if you also do business with his suppliers or subcontractors. Or perhaps one of your plants can let him have the spare part he needs to get back into production. Even your traffic department may be able to help by figuring out faster ways of getting goods from his sources to him, or from him to you.

On really big orders, you may want to have suppliers submit progress reports. These could be either narrative comments on how the work is going, or PERT or CPM charts identifying the various activities that suppliers are simultaneously engaged in to complete your orders.

Discipline at both ends of the purchasing cycle—at the buyer's end and at the supplier's end—is what it takes to make expediting work. As the man in the middle, you're in the best position to impose that discipline in a realistic and workable fashion.

33

VENDOR RATING MADE EASY

A lot of controversy has arisen in the purchasing profession in recent years as to the worth of formal programs for evaluating suppliers.

Those in favor of such programs (and many of them come from big companies involved in defense work and other government projects) claim that a highly structured approach to vendor rating is a must.

Those opposed to such programs (many of them from smaller firms that have been subjected to the bigger companies' rating plans) say that formal vendor rating is a waste of time.

As a buyer, you may be a bit confused as to which of these theories is closest to the mark. You may recognize that vendor rating is an integral part of your job—something you do every time you add a new source to a bidders' list, or award an order—and you may want some sort of planned program to supplement your own intuitive judgments. At the same time, you probably don't want to set up a rating system that's too elaborate, or one that entirely supplants your own subjective opinions.

If you're in this position, take just a minute to consider the purposes of the two main types of vendor rating: evaluation of prospective suppliers, and of those with whom you're already doing business.

Quite probably, this analysis of the objectives of vendor rating will result in your deciding on two questions that you'll want answered:

In rating potential suppliers, the question will be: "Can this firm perform satisfactorily for my company?" When the answer is affirmative, you'll probably want to solicit quotes from the firm—possibly starting with less critical items and building up to more important items as you gain actual experience with the source.

In rating current suppliers, the question will be: "How well is this firm performing for my company?" Based on the answer, you can (1) award the appropriate amount of new business to the supplier, and (2) identify problem areas where he needs help and guidance.

Here are a few suggestions on how you can come up with the answers to these two questions, without building up too complex a rating program:

In rating prospective suppliers, you can get a pretty good idea of the company in question by looking at just a few factors. These would include:

(a) Management attitude
(b) Financial status
(c) Personnel qualifications
(d) Physical plant and layout
(e) Manufacturing and test equipment
(f) Labor history
(g) Relations with customers
(h) Systems for purchasing, quality control, production control, etc.

In most cases, you can rate factors like these as simply acceptable or non-acceptable. If all eight factors for a firm are acceptable, then the company is obviously a good bet to add to the bidders' list. If all eight are unacceptable, it's equally clearcut that you won't want to go near the company—let alone buy from it. If some factors are rated acceptable and others are rated unacceptable, you at least have some basis for coming up with a buy or no-buy decision. You'll have the facts, and can make up your own mind accordingly.

You may feel that the eight factors listed aren't enough to look at in considering potential suppliers. If so, add a few: whatever you think are pertinent. But don't get suckered into a position where you have 1,001 categories, sub-categories, and sub-sub-categories on which you're trying to appraise potential sources. You'll simply confuse things for yourself. The same holds true for the scores you set up for measuring the various factors. If you stray too far from the yes-no principle of acceptable *vs* non-acceptable, you may get into trouble. How can you possibly measure the differences between a company's management attitude —or any other characteristic—being "excellent," "very good," or "good"? The lines of distinction simply aren't definite enough.

As far as rating current suppliers is concerned, there are just three questions you have to answer at the outset.

The first question is a "who" question: what suppliers should a regular rating system cover? The answer to this is any major suppliers of your choice. And a major supplier might be one meeting any of the following qualifications: high dollar volume of business, large number of individual orders, or critical nature of the parts/services supplied.

The second question is a "when" question: how often should you recap various suppliers' scores under a rating system? The best bet here is probably quarterly—this being a period of time that allows enough experience to be built up to indicate performance trends, and also allows corrective action to be taken without too long a delay.

The final question is a "how" question—how can an individual buyer set up a vendor rating program without going off the deep end with formulas and lots of paperwork?

Step one in answering this question is to realize that a good vendor rating system is not geared to measure the traditional three factors: quality, service and price. The reason is that quality and service cannot be measured in the same context as price—nor can price be measured in the same context as quality and service. Quality and service performance can (and should be) measured long-term, and price is simply a quantitative absolute that exists on any bid or order. It is just there, that's all.

In practical terms, this means that a good vendor rating system measures quality and service—and applies the measurements gained to the determination of whether or not a price is justified, competitive, or equitable. Once this determination has been made on any particular order or quotation, that's the end of the matter. There is no real need to record "price performance" as part of a vendor rating program.

A better plan, if you want a realistic method of rating current vendors, is to spin off another "service" category so that you have a system for rating (a) quality performance, (b) delivery service, (c) technical service.

It's not hard to come up with a plan for rating these three areas. To rate quality performance, you can use either percent of lots accepted, or percent of parts or pieces accepted. Under this system, a supplier who had an 85% acceptance score (on whichever basis you want) would have a quality score of 85. Or you can work it backwards if you want to—using percent of parts or lots rejected as the criterion. (Some people feel more comfortable, apparently, with rating systems where low numbers represent good scores.)

To rate delivery performance, take the percentage of on-time (or late) deliveries, and translate it into a similar score for on-time delivery service. You can either penalize suppliers for early shipments, or treat these ahead-of-schedule deliveries as though they actually had come in as requested.

To translate the amount of technical service a supplier gives you into a rating score, add up the dollar savings that his ideas have been responsible for. (As noted in the following chapter, your production department can probably give you a big assist in determining how much credit a supplier deserves for new ideas and suggestions.)

If you want to come up with some sort of percentage for the technical-service score, there are two approaches you can use. One is to divide each supplier's dollar savings by the dollar value of the business awarded him during the rating period. Another is to divide his dollar savings by the total dollar savings credited to all vendors during the period.

If you use either of these approaches, you'll get a percentage that you can then add to the other two percentages so you can average them all out.

It's probably safer, however, to shy away from over-all averages on vendor rating programs. What you really want to know is simply this: how reliable the supplier is on delivery and quality, and how much imagination he's using in solving your problems. If you keep a sheet on each major supplier, listing his performance in each rating area, you'll be able to spot trends up or down. You can zero in on the areas where he needs help in helping you. And that—not the search for a master formula that will unfailingly rank your suppliers from best to worst—is what vendor rating is all about.

34

ASK PRODUCTION TO HELP RATE SUPPLIERS

The production department can be a buyer's strongest ally when it comes to rating suppliers. A good production manager knows exactly what's going on in the shop at all times. He and his staff can give the buyer a highly practical viewpoint on anything pertaining to purchased goods: materials, machines, parts, components or supplies.

The reason is simple. The production department is the place where everything has to come together—in the right quantities, at the right time, and of the right quality—to produce the buying company's end products. Even a slight miscue can at least temporarily put the firm out of business—or drive its costs, and the production manager, right up the wall.

Because the typical production manager shoulders such a big responsibility, he is usually intensely interested in everything affecting his department. And while the cigar-chomping bull-of-the-woods production supervisor has largely been replaced by more sophisticated, engineering-trained managers, there are still very few occasions when purchasing doesn't hear about it when something goes wrong.

Examples: a late delivery that's threatening to close down a line; a supposedly supplier-certified shipment that's loaded with rejects; a balky machine; excessive scrap; etc.

When such situations occur, the production manager usually—and quite rightly—gets hold of the buyer to have them straightened out. This kind of communication is okay for after-the-fact problem solving. But it's far better for production and purchasing to work together on supplier rating in advance.

If they do, both departments will benefit. Production will be assured of a chance to present its opinions on suppliers' capabilities. Purchasing can use those opinions—which are exceptionally broad in scope —to supplement its own observations.

For example, a buyer may be faced with a situation where production output on a certain machine isn't meeting expectations. The machine may be turning out fewer parts per hour than was originally estimated, or the operator may be having a tough time holding tolerances.

In such cases, it's often difficult to pinpoint responsibilities. Is it the fault of the machine? The tooling? The raw material that's being processed? For a completely unbiased opinion—regardless of the various suppliers' claims and counter-claims—the buyer should ask production. The production manager knows from experience what similar machines can do with similar materials.

For best results, this same know-how should be brought to bear on supplier evaluation early in the game. As in any vendor evaluation program, it should be applied to the appraisal of both potential and current suppliers.

Here's a brief rundown on the areas where production knowledge can be of particular help in rating suppliers on two important classes of purchased items.

In helping the buyer rate potential suppliers of machinery and other capital goods, the production manager can provide a detailed picture of what will happen in production if a particular unit is purchased. He can analyze the net effect on productivity in quantitative terms: parts per hour or per day, etc.

At the same time, he can zero in on such allied factors as ease of machine operation, time needed to train operators, labor availability and wage rates. If necessary, he's just the man to visit other firms currently using various brands of equipment. During such visits, or through his professional associations, he can find out how well various units perform once they're installed.

The production manager will probably take a somewhat different approach in evaluating potential suppliers of parts and materials.

In such cases, he will want to spend more time in suppliers' plants, rather than in those of their other customers. (If he doesn't, the buyer should encourage him to.)

During such visits, perhaps while the buyer is closeted with the supplier's sales manager, the production manager can get out in the shop to see what makes things tick. He can get together with the supplier's production head, quality control supervisor, and other technical people. He can size up the production operations from every angle: the efficiency of material flow, the quality of general housekeeping, the age, condition and capacity of machines, the experience of the workers, etc.

As part of such on-the-spot inspections, the production manager can spell out just what's going to happen to the supplier's parts or materials in his own shop. This will eliminate confusion on specs or tolerances. And, if the production manager sums up all his observations for the buyer in a written report, the buyer will be that much ahead of the game in rating the supplier.

In evaluating a current supplier of machinery, the main question the production manager will seek to answer is: "Has this unit lived up to what we expected of it?" There are other questions that naturally follow. Among them: Did the installation of the machine unnecessarily disrupt production? Were there any unforeseen installation costs that we weren't warned about? Did the operator training program go as smoothly as expected? Has the supplier been cooperative in making any emergency repairs—or in supplying maintenance manuals or spare parts?

In rating current suppliers of parts and materials, by contrast, the emphasis will probably be on technical service. The reason for this is that quality control catches most quality problems, and purchasing's expediting section is well aware of delivery problems.

The production manager, in other words, can pinpoint the suppliers whose salesmen are just order-takers—and those whose sales reps have a genuine interest in improving product quality and in lowering costs.

In many cases, for example, a salesman may suggest minor changes in material or processes—changes that without affecting quality will help production cut its expenses drastically. Or in other cases the changes may pertain to ordering quantity, storage or handling methods, etc.

As the one who's most directly affected by such efficiencies, the production manager is in the best position to inform purchasing of how the changes came about. He's the one who knows how credit for the ideas should be apportioned.

Ideally, then, the production manager should sit in on all supplier rating sessions. Because of the pressures of time, this may not always be possible as a practical matter. One compromise approach is to have the production manager endorse the buyer's supplier ratings before they become final. This saves the production manager time, but gives him a chance to recommend changes in any ratings that he thinks are out of line.

35

SUPPLIERS' IDEAS PAY OFF

One of the biggest frustrations a buyer must face is the situation where his suppliers don't come up with workable ideas that his company can put to practical use.

A buyer in this position knows that there's a wealth of know-how and experience in vendor firms. Each of these companies is a specialist in its field. It should be able to suggest all sorts of ideas for improving product quality, lowering costs, or otherwise improving efficiency. And it should be able to do so consistently, not just once in a while.

If you're in such a position—one where supplier suggestions aren't coming in as frequently as they should—perhaps you should mount a campaign to get things rolling. To do so, you must recognize three steps that are needed:

1. You have to identify your company's needs.
2. You have to communicate these needs to suppliers.
3. You have to motivate your suppliers to become members of the problem-solving team.

To identify your company's needs in specific terms, you have to get together with the people in your company who can define their current problems. This means working with production on material specifications and problems pertaining to equipment; with design engineers on component or assembly designs; with material handling specialists on material flow matters; with marketing on competitive-price problems that may be bothering them; with the office manager or systems people on administrative bottlenecks; etc.

A good way to start is to sit down with each of these individuals and ask them to define just one current problem that they would like to have solved. You may get a few facetious answers. But by and large the replies will tend to reflect the priorities that each operating department has assigned—even if informally—to its current problems.

In such discussions, it's important to nail down specifics. If someone tells you his biggest problem is "high material costs," don't let it go at that. Ask him to identify just one material where he feels the current price isn't justified, or where the use of alternate materials appears even vaguely possible.

As you talk with the operating people, keep in mind that this is only step one of your campaign to enlist supplier help. The next step is communicating your current problems to the vendors. Keep asking yourself this question: "Do I now have enough specific information to pass along?" If you do this, you'll avoid situations where the only thing you can say to suppliers is something like this: "Well, we're in the pump business, and we'd appreciate any ideas you might have about pumps. . . ."

The second step—communicating specific needs to suppliers—is something that has to be handled on a continuing basis. There are many ways to do this.

One way (and it's one that requires the cooperation of your boss and the boss's boss) is to hold an open house for suppliers. This means inviting all major suppliers in for a day or half a day, and giving them the word on the creative and innovative effort that's expected of them. Quite typically, the company president or chairman of the board will be the lead-off speaker at such open houses. Then the suppliers are broken into groups who can get together with buyers and operating personnel, for specific discussions of current problems.

If your company ever holds a supplier open house, chances are you'll be picked to host one of the discussion groups. Make the most of the opportunity. Get together in advance with your group's co-hosts from other departments, and work out at least a tentative list of what should be covered in the talks with your supplier guests.

Another useful technique is to set up value analysis exhibits either in purchasing's reception room, or along the corridors leading to the purchasing department. Such exhibits can really dramatize the practical results that VA brings.

Most VA exhibits are keyed to a "before-and-after" theme. They show actual samples of parts or other purchased items, where supplier assistance has been instrumental in improving value. Each set of samples is usually labeled with a notice highlighting unit savings and total annual savings.

As part of a VA exhibit—or separately, if desired—samples of other items, where supplier help is especially wanted, can be displayed. On items that are currently being produced in-house, "meet-or-beat" price tags can be hung. The prices represent the costs for making the items in-plant, and give the suppliers specific targets to shoot for in framing their own ideas on furnishing them as subcontracted items.

Perhaps your management won't want to set up a formal VA or problem-parts exhibit. But you can still apply the same principles on your own. Keep a few samples in your desk: of items that have already been successfully value analyzed, and of ones where you'd like new ideas from salesmen. Bring them out when you're talking with salesmen. Use them to dramatize what you're looking for in the way of suggestions.

Also, even if your company doesn't authorize a full-scale supplier open house, you can make any salesman's or technical rep's visit an un-official plant tour. Take him out to meet the people with the problems. Give him a chance to see the situations that you think he can correct.

The third step in your campaign—motivating suppliers to come up with ideas—is one that depends on your own ingenuity and sincerity.

For example, your company's request for quote forms may be printed with a note soliciting vendor ideas and alternate proposals. The same message may be on the postage-meter used to imprint purchasing's outgoing mail. There is nothing wrong with these techniques, but the problem is that such notices tend to become routine. They're there all the time, and after a while suppliers may not even notice them.

To overcome this problem, try varying the methods you use to so-licit suppliers' ideas. Make up a new form letter every once in a while, or a postcard. Try to get someone from the art department to dream up a few cartoons that will get your message across more vigorously than straight text. Use all the ingenuity you can in developing new ways to get your message across.

At the same time, make it obvious that you're sincere about want-ing supplier help. Here are several ways you can do this:

Follow through on the ideas that suppliers do submit to you. Acknowledge them when they're first proposed—in writing if they seem workable and worthy of further investigation.

Keep after the engineers, technicians or other staffers who will explore the feasibility of new materials, methods or processes. Don't let them delay the test programs unnecessarily—either from lassitude or lack of interest.

See to it that the proposals get a fair test—one that's not weighted in favor of existing methods. Question test procedures and criteria if they don't seem reasonable.

Keep suppliers posted on the results of tests. And advise them of any delays that may have come up since their submission of the proposals.

Most important of all, reward the suppliers who come up with ideas that your company can use profitably. This is the most important part of motivating suppliers to come up with additional ideas in the future—and it's also one of the most difficult. It takes a great deal of judgment.

(Your company may have a formal program which includes VA incentive contracts for suppliers. These contracts state in advance how the supplier and the customer will share the savings resulting from supplier ideas. But chances are, though, that you as buyer will in most cases have to determine how the supplier is to be rewarded for his creative effort on your behalf.)

You can't look for absolute guidelines, either. The rule of giving the supplier who came up with the idea the first order—and then soliciting competition on future orders—has serious weaknesses. In many cases, the first order is a trial order, appreciably smaller than the quantities later ordered for volume production.

Instead, you have to sit down and make a judgment based on your own common sense and the facts available to you. You have to ask yourself questions like these:

How new was the vendor's idea? Was it a brand-new and completely innovative concept—or a modification of existing technology? Would anyone else probably have come up with the idea in the near future? Or would it never have come to light except for the supplier's application of his know-how? How much time did the supplier spend in developing it? Did he have any out-of-pocket expenses? What will the idea save us annually? Can we apply the same basic idea to other parts and processes? Are there supplementary benefits we gain from the idea: improved quality in addition to lower costs, easier maintenance in addition to increased production?

Based on the answers to questions like these, you should be able to determine how to reward a supplier for his ideas. You may want to give him the current order, a series of orders, or simply give him a crack at a larger share of your business in general. But, whatever your decision, it will be fair to everyone concerned: your company, the supplier, and your other suppliers.

It's not easy. But it's one of the most important parts of your job.

PART FIVE

Training and Self-Development

Every businessman has a double obligation—to himself and to his company—to continually broaden his horizons. Executive education is not a finite something that comes packed inside a rolled-up sheepskin— whether the degree in question is a B.S. in engineering, an A.B. in psychology, or an M.B.A. from the most prestigious university in the country. It is, or should be, a continuing and ongoing process through which the individual adds to his knowledge, improves his professional stature, and increases his value to his company.

This principle applies to businessmen in all functions of a company's operations: engineering, marketing, personnel, finance, etc. But for buyers it has a rather special meaning and application. There are two reasons why:

1. The buyer's efforts within the company have a direct influence on profits.

2. The buyer's activities are strongly influenced by external forces in the outside world.

How well the buyer does his job will often be translated straight to the bottom line of the corporate balance sheet. And the impact of outside events—the development of new technologies, new marketing strategies, and new distribution methods—will inevitably shape the nature of the buyer's decisions.

To put it still another way, the scope of options available to any buyer is continually expanding. Yesterday's answers won't suffice for tomorrow's questions. No buyer can afford to be complacent about what he knows.

As a result, buyers must continually keep up with what's happening in their industries, their technologies, their markets. At the same time they must keep up with new methods for applying what they know—by making the most effective use of general management skills and tools.

The following chapters discuss some of the ways in which buyers can meet the dual challenge of training and self-development.

36

BUYER TRAINING IS THE BUYER'S JOB

Training other buyers may not be part of your formal job description, but chances are that this task will be dropped squarely in your lap at some time during your buying career.

How well you handle this quasi-official duty will be a direct indication, to your boss, of your responsibility, tact, executive ability and willingness to help the entire department.

Think back to your first day on the job—whether it was 10 years, 10 months, or 10 days ago. If your company is like most firms, your indoctrination to actual on-the-job buying probably started with the P.A. taking you out to your desk, introducing you to the buyer next to you—and telling him to show you the ropes.

There's nothing wrong with this approach. Department heads just don't have time to shepherd new employees through training programs. In addition, they may not be 100% familiar with procedural details—even though they themselves developed the procedures' prototypes years before.

The reason for this is that procedures (especially in their more routine aspects) tend to adapt themselves to current operating conditions.
Thus, even though departmental or corporate policy may remain un-
changed, an experienced buyer may be better qualified than the P.A. to
answer questions about the mechanics of running the department.

Typical examples: How are incoming requisitions logged in? What's
the exact routing for various parts of the p.o. and other multi-part forms?

So, if the P.A. selects you to train a new staff member, don't gripe
about the extra time you'll have to spend. You should look on the assignment as a challenge, and—if you approach it in an organized way—
you'll probably learn as much as the new man.

In explaining departmental systems or your own methods for handling paperwork, you may even discover some improved techniques.
The trainee will probably have a disconcerting habit of asking "Why do
you do it like this?"—if he doesn't, you should encourage him to—and
the only response to some of these queries may be "Because we've always done it this way."

If so, you have probably spotted a systems step that can be modified
or even eliminated.

Let's assume that P.A. Smith has brought Harry the trainee out to
your desk, has told you that he's "a new member of the department,"
and has asked you to fill him in on how the purchasing department works.

Do you immediately start firing a mass of facts at Harry? Not at
all. The first thing you do is ask Harry to wait at your desk for a few
minutes, while you follow Mr. Smith back to his office. First, you should
get the background information you'll need in order to set up a first-rate
training program for Harry.

In this preliminary session with Mr. Smith, you should find out just
what types of item Harry is slated to handle as well as the timing for
the training. If Harry is an addition to the staff, there will probably be
no fixed target date for completion of his indoctrination. But if he's a
replacement for a buyer who's leaving, you will have to drill him in his
duties more rapidly.

Harry's background should also be covered in your meeting with
Mr. Smith, so that you can find out whether or not he has any previous
purchasing experience, technical commodity knowledge, etc. Finally, you
should ask how much detail he has already given Harry on company and
departmental policy.

Then, when you rejoin Harry at your desk, the first thing you should
do is ask him if he has any questions regarding policy matters.

The reason for this is that Harry may well have questions—many of
them—even if Mr. Smith thinks the policy area has already been well

covered. Often a new employee will be reluctant to quiz the boss too closely on matters that aren't completely clear to him. A fellow staff-member, on the other hand, isn't quite so awe-inspiring—so you're in an excellent position to thrash out misunderstandings and clear up ambiguities.

Moreover, it's only fair to the new man to let him in on the "unwritten rules" of the department regarding matters such as dress, decorum, and length of lunch hours. Also, if the trainee has moved from another town, it's an especially nice gesture to fill him in on the quality of local eating places, the location of shops for on-the-way-home purchases, and other personal matters that he'll find useful.

The first step in the actual training program should also be keyed to a personal theme: the introduction of the trainee to those he'll be working with. And whether you're introducing him to other members of the purchasing department, shop personnel or suppliers—make sure that each person gets the other's name, and gets it right.

If your department has a manual of purchasing procedures, you're that much ahead of the game in setting up a training schedule. Depending on the size and scope of the manual, you may want to give the trainee a day or two of "assigned reading." Then, in question-and-answer sessions, you can interpret any sections of the manual that have posed difficulties for the trainee.

If you don't have a manual, the best bet is to give the new man a verbal outline of what you think should be in a manual if you did have one. This may take time. But laying the groundwork in this manner will in the long run shorten the training period.

It's also important to remember, in training a buyer, that the buying job involves two main types of duties: semi-clerical and creative. Depending on the trainee's background, you will have to emphasize one or the other of these areas.

For example, if the new man has purchasing experience in another company, he presumably knows something about creative buying. Your job, consequently, will be to drill him in the paperwork procedures of your department.

If, on the other hand, you're training an expediter from your own department to be a buyer, he probably knows the clerical routines already. You can concentrate on more advanced matters.

Explaining the paperwork details of purchasing to a new man, naturally, is the easier of the two jobs. As the old adage for speech-makers puts it, the best way of getting the message across is to "tell them what you're going to tell them, tell them—and then tell them what you told them." Adapting this routine to buyer training, you should tell the man what you're going to show him, show him—and then tell him what you showed him.

This more-or-less mechanical approach is especially well-suited to instructions on how to edit a requisition for order-typing; how to set up follow-up files on quotation requests or open orders; how to prepare a recap of bids; etc.

When you think the trainee has grasped the system, have him go through the routine under your close supervision. After a few such sessions, he should know not only what he's doing, but why he's doing it.

For more sophisticated aspects of purchasing—such as interviewing vendors and working with using departments on cost reduction ideas —you can use an adaptation of the show-tell method.

A good idea here is to have the trainee sit in on all interviews you conduct. Then, when you and he are alone after the interview, you should point out why (and how) you directed the discussion as you did. At this time, while the meeting is still fresh in both your minds, you should encourage him to ask questions—and answer them frankly.

If you arrange for him to audit both vendor interviews and sessions with operating personnel, you will give him the broad background he needs to handle all aspects of the buying job.

After he's attended a few interviews as a silent partner, you should then allow him to participate—and, finally, to run a meeting himself with you sitting in as an observer.

Patience, tact—and the ability to be specific in your criticism—will help you immeasurably in training other buyers. If you cultivate these attributes, and accept the assignment as a means of broadening your own knowledge and experience—both you and your pupil will benefit.

37

THE BUYER AND SELF–DEVELOPMENT

Every buyer should have some sort of self-development program mapped out. It needn't be an elaborate affair involving charts, graphs and timetables of accomplishments. But it should be tailored to the buyer's own current position, his strengths and weaknesses, and long-range objectives.

This is true not only for small-company buyers, who may have to depend solely on their own efforts for self-improvement. It's also true for big-company buyers whose training may be monitored, on a continuing basis, as part of a formal personnel development program.

For no training counselor can possibly do more than *assist* in an employee's evaluation of his job progress. The ultimate motivation for professional growth must come from within the individual. It must be based on candid self-appraisal.

In practical terms, a buyer's first step in establishing a self-development program should be to re-examine his long-range goals. He should decide—at least on a tentative basis—just what course he wants his professional career to follow. Only then can he set up short-range goals, based on his current status, to pace himself toward his ultimate objective.

Here are a few typical questions that a buyer might ask himself to help crystallize his long-term goals:

Am I in purchasing for the long haul, or is the buying job simply a means of broadening my general business background?

If I do intend to make purchasing my career, where do I want to be "X" years from now?

Am I aiming for a management slot?

Should it involve direct buying supervision?

Would I prefer a staff management responsibility, such as purchasing research?

Or would I rather remain in a buyer's post, where I can devote myself to becoming an expert on just a few markets, industries, materials, or manufacturing processes?

Once the answers to these questions have been defined, the buyer should take stock of his own situation and of his own capabilities. His aim should be to determine just how likely his chances of reaching his ultimate goal are. This means an objective appraisal is necessary.

For example, in considering his position in his present company, the buyer will have to take a look at his own age, and at the ages of the head of purchasing and of his own immediate supervisor. He'll also have to analyze his progress to date, as measured both by salary advances and by the amount of authority that has been delegated to him. Finally, he'll have to gauge the opportunities for advancement, as dictated by his firm's promotion policies.

But even more important is the self-appraisal that must accompany this evaluation of external forces. Even in a situation where job growth seems stymied, the buyer can tap all sorts of resources for long-range self-development.

In general, these resources cover three areas: technical, commercial, and personal. The buyer's next step in framing a do-it-yourself training program, therefore, should be to determine the areas he's weak in. Then he can establish appropriate priorities for improving his knowledge and skills.

In the technical area, the buyer might want to bone up on general production techniques and assembly systems, on material characteristics, and on the manufacturing methods used for his own company's product line.

Much of this know-how can be obtained through shop visits and daily contact with requisitioners. In addition, the buyer should make the most of chances to attend trade shows, to visit vendors' plants, and to talk with suppliers' technical people.

In most localities, the career-minded buyer can find university extension courses or evening high school courses that fit in with his self-development plans. For example, many schools offer courses in blue-print reading. Even where local institutions don't offer pertinent courses, the buyer can turn to correspondence schools or the town library. (Don't hesitate to ask librarians for suggestions in setting up a self-help reading program; chances are they'll be delighted to work with you on your project.)

Reading programs and extension courses can also be invaluable in improving commercial knowledge. In this area, the emphasis should be on contract law, finance, accounting, inventory and production control, statistics, marketing, economics, quality control, etc.

A good way to find out what courses are offered by mail in these subjects is to write the National Home Study Council, 1601 18th St., N.W., Washington, D.C. 20009. The NHSC is a non-profit public service organization which regularly screens the nation's private home study schools. It analyzes each school's educational objectives, instructional materials and methods, faculty, attention to individual students' differences, etc. Then twice a year it publishes a directory of accredited schools, with an index of subjects taught.

Other organizations which publish educational material and hold seminars on commercial subjects include these:

THE NATIONAL ASSOCIATION OF PURCHASING MANAGEMENT, 11 Park Place, New York, N.Y. (There are also local chapters of NAPM throughout the country.)

THE AMERICAN MANAGEMENT ASSOCIATION, 135 W. 50th St., New York, N.Y.

THE ADMINISTRATIVE MANAGEMENT SOCIETY, Willow Grove, Pa.

AMERICAN SOCIETY FOR TRAINING AND DEVELOPMENT, Box 5307, Madison, Wis.

SOCIETY FOR THE ADVANCEMENT OF MANAGEMENT, 1472 Broadway, New York, N.Y.

AMERICAN PRODUCTION & INVENTORY CONTROL SOCIETY, Watergate Bldg., 2600 Virginia Ave., N.W., Washington, D.C.

DATA PROCESSING MANAGEMENT ASSOCIATION, 505 Busse Highway, Park Ridge, Ill.

SYSTEMS AND PROCEDURES ASSOCIATION, 24587 Bagley St., Cleveland, O.

Finally—or, preferably, simultaneously with beefing up his technical and commercial knowledge—the buyer should seek to develop the personal attributes that are vital in the purchasing job.

This is in many ways the toughest part of self-development—for two very good reasons. First, it's much more difficult to be objective about one's personal weaknesses than it is to admit lack of knowledge on a specific subject. Second, although some literature and formal courses are available as development guides, most training in this area must necessarily be on an informal basis.

A buyer can start by taking a close look at how he stacks up on neatness, grooming, decorum, poise, tact, communications skill, planning ability, perseverance, imagination, and acceptance of responsibility. Then, once he has identified his shortcomings, he can take steps to correct them.

Much of this corrective action will take place on a day-to-day basis in the office. It's there, in the countless contacts with requisitioners, suppliers and others, that the buyer can practice his skill in human relations. Also it's in the office that the buyer can observe just how the department head and other supervisors handle some of the ticklish problems that arise in purchasing. (Even if they're weak in this area, the buyer can still learn by seeing how they mishandle sticky situations.)

But, over and above the practice that he gets in the office, the buyer can also use extra-curricular activities to polish up his skill in working with people.

By being active in church, school or civic affairs, and by taking part in service clubs, scouting or other community activities, the buyer can gain much valuable experience.

Know-how garnered from such activities can range from public speaking to meeting leadership; from principles of finance to public relations techniques.

The degree to which the buyer applies this know-how back on the job will to a great extent determine how successful his self-development program is going to be.

38

MAKE THE MOST OF YOUR TIME

Skillful use of time is the hallmark of a good executive. With only so many minutes in each working day, a manager has to make the most of every millisecond. And buyers, if they're to be true business managers of their commodities, must learn to squeeze a wide variety of projects into every day at the office.

The reason is simple. Although a buyer's basic responsibility can be summed up easily—"get reliable goods in on time at competitive prices"—100% fulfillment of that responsibility isn't easy. It often involves time-consuming negotiations, interviews with salesmen, field trips, get-togethers with personnel from other departments, etc.

It's no wonder that "lack of time" is one of the complaints most often voiced by industrial buyers. And because of the nature of the buying job, it's especially dangerous when a buyer doesn't have enough time or doesn't make full use of the time he does have.

The usual reason for such a situation is the buyer's devoting a disproportionate amount of time to the routine parts of his job: getting requisitions processed and purchase orders issued. He knows that everyone involved—from the purchasing manager to other department heads—will take a dim view of a paperwork backlog. He's thus impelled to get the clerical work done at all costs—and therefore the more creative parts of his job suffer.

Right now is when you should try to get out of the lack-of-time bind, if you are in it. It's not always easy, but with a little perseverance it can be done.

First, make an analysis of the way you spend each working day. This doesn't mean keeping an exact log of your daily activities, and plotting what you're doing every 15 minutes or so. It does mean making an honest effort to see if you have enough time for your job—and if there are any activities that take more time than they should.

The best way to do this is simply to ask yourself a couple of questions at the end of each day:

1. Did I get everything done today that I had planned?
2. If I didn't, what were the reasons?

If you jot down the reasons every day, you'll build up a meaningful list after several weeks. It should show you obstacles that interfere with the best use of your time. It might show, for example, that you're spending a great deal of time in quality control, trying to solve reject problems. Or the list might indicate that production control's repeated calls for delivery speed-ups are keeping you glued to the phone for long intervals.

Whatever the reason, you can then take corrective action. If quality problems are continually tying you up, you might want to make a wholesale switch in vendors. If production control is the culprit, you should ask that department to reassess all its delivery requirements in advance and thus avoid emergency calls.

Once you have identified the problems that are costing you valuable time, and have taken concrete steps to solve them, you can then zero in on other areas: those daily activities where control of the time spent is largely in your own hands.

The first rule here—and it's one that often gets more lip-service than actual practice—is to delegate every task that doesn't require your personal attention. If you have a secretary, buying assistant or expediter who can handle routine duties, don't hesitate to turn the work over to them. If you cling to routine matters, you'll never get out from under the clerical burden.

It may be, of course, that you don't have such assistants on a formal basis. Even when this is the case, you can still delegate by other means. Some of these have already been discussed in other sections of this book, but they're worth repeating.

For example, you can set up methods under which using departments write their own releases against blanket orders and contracts. You can also legitimately ask supplier salesmen to handle much of the paperwork in listing requirements, pricing various items, etc.

Another useful trick is to use what might be called the "systems approach" for all communications inside and outside the company. Use forms, form letters and printed notices to get your messages across.

For trimming the time spent in initial interviews with salesmen, for example, a printed or typed-up statement of your company's basic buying policies would be invaluable. Perhaps your firm already has a welcome booklet covering matters such as purchasing policies. But if it doesn't, there's no reason why you couldn't have a brief notice outlining your own buying policies typed up. The alternative is to rehash the same data verbally with every new salesman who calls on you—and that's just the kind of situation that consumes precious minutes.

As a buyer, you also have to be somewhat aggressive in husbanding your available time. You can't afford to be the "nice guy" who handles personal purchases as a favor. And you must insist that incoming requisitions be readable, complete and accurate. If you start sending garbled requisitions back to the originators for clarification, rather than trying to decipher them at your end, you can probably save a great deal of time.

In addition, you should guard against situations where you're tempted to save five minutes that will later cost you several hours or more of time and effort.

Example: a persistent salesman is trying to get you to accept a sample of his goods. The easy way out may be to accept it, simply to get rid of him in a hurry. But, by accepting the sample, you're then committed to run tests, record results, keep him posted, etc. Best bet in such a situation is to stick to your guns even if it does take a few extra minutes to pry him and his sample out of your office.

As part of your campaign to save time, you should also plan ahead, anticipate time-consuming projects that are likely to hit your desk, and make every effort to stagger the delivery dates of such projects. You should establish blanket order dates, for instance, so that just a few agreements come up for renegotiation each month during the year. Or, if your firm has a traditionally slack period, you should schedule contract negotiations, plant visits, and other special projects for that time.

In addition—just as you "pool" requirements by covering several requisitions with one p.o.—you can in many cases pool daily activities. This means making the maximum use of every interview, internal or external, by discussing all important matters still unresolved between you and your visitor.

If you make a real effort to do so, you can probably make better use of your time and become more valuable to your company in the process. But, since it's bad psychology to start such a program with a big backlog of unfinished work, your very first step should be to try to catch up and get current on your duties.

If you do have a big backlog, you'd better look it over carefully. Establish priorities on what has to be done first, and weed out any jobs that you can turn over to an assistant. Set yourself some overtime work if you have to.

In extreme cases, you may want to check with your boss, to see if another buyer can help you get caught up. Then, with your desk cleared for action, you should be able to demonstrate that you mean it when you say that you're going to "make the most of your time" in the future.

39

GETTING READY FOR EDP

Sooner or later, if it hasn't already happened, your boss is going to call you into his office and tell you that your company's purchasing systems are about to be computerized. The plan may be to use a company-owned or leased computer, or to rent EDP time at a service bureau or time-sharing outfit. But whatever the set-up, you're going to have to live with a computer.

Your reaction when you get the news will undoubtedly depend on how much factual experience you've had with electronic data processing, and on what friends (especially any in the buying fraternity) have told you.

If you are indifferent or hostile to the thought of working with a computer every day, the reason may be that you expect the new arrangement to dehumanize you and your job. You may even view it as a threat to your job security.

If this is the case, the first thing you'd better do is get rid of any such preconceived notions. Far from dehumanizing the buyer's role, the computer puts an even greater premium on human brainpower and judgment. It frees the buyer of much detail work, and gives him time for planning. It gives him more time for decision making, and provides him with the kind of data he needs for choosing among alternate courses of action.

For example, the computer can identify groups of items warranting pooled orders or annual contracts; it can pinpoint likely candidates for cost reduction study; and it can print out bid analyses a hundred ways from Sunday. But without the buyer's interpretation of such data, the information simply cannot be used.

Perhaps you're already looking forward to what the computer can do to make you a better buyer. If so, you're one step ahead of the game. But even if you do have an open mind on this score, there are certain steps you can take to get the most out of EDP.

In general, try to learn as much as you can about computers: what they are, what they can do, and what they can't do. Although you don't need an in-depth knowledge of programming and other software elements, you should understand the basic guidelines on which programs and systems are built.

One way to get this kind of know-how is to sign up for evening extension courses, home study schooling, or seminars run by computer manufacturers. You can also learn a lot by picking the brains of company programmers and system analysts assigned to put purchasing on the computer.

One basic area that you should be familiar with, simply because it's such an integral part of all computer operations, is the kind of mathematics the big brains use. (The information will also be helpful to you if you're struggling to help your children with their new-math homework involving "bases" other than the traditional decimal system.)

Unlike the decimal system (which was developed because humans have 10 fingers to count on) computers use binary digits—"bits" in the jargon of the EDP trade. And the binary digit system is "base two," just as the decimal system is "base 10."

The computer has to use a binary system—which depends on the use of zeroes and ones to represent all numbers—because a machine can recognize only yes-no terms. A switch has to be either open or shut; a magnetic current has to flow in one direction or the other; there can't be any in-betweens.

To see how the binary system works, take a look at Fig. 25, which compares the value of place positions in both binary and decimal systems.

The important thing to remember is that the various place posi-

				VALUES OF PLACE POSITIONS					
	n^8	n^7	n^6	n^5	n^4	n^3	n^2	n^1	n^0
Binary System (Base Two; $n=2$)	256	128	64	32	16	8	4	2	1
Decimal-System (Base Ten; $n=10$)	100,000,000	10,000,000	1,000,000	100,000	10,000	1,000	100	10	1

Fig. 25 Binary mathematics, the computer's basic digital system, is based on the use of zeroes and ones to represent all numbers. Table above shows how binary place positions' values correspond to those of the conventional decimal (base 10) system.

tions of any numbering system represent powers of "n"—the base number of the system. The far right column is n to the zero power—which is always equal to 1—and each column to the left is n to one greater power. In a binary system, these are powers of 2.

Thus the decimal number 5 would be expressed as 101 in the binary system—the digits representing $(1 \times 4) + (0 \times 2) + (1 \times 1)$. Or the decimal number 9 would be 1001: $(1 \times 8) + (0 \times 4) + (0 \times 2) + (1 \times 1)$.

In addition to learning the basic language of EDP, the buyer who's about to be computerized should be prepared to be patient during the changeover period from manual systems. No matter how carefully planned an EDP system is, there's always a certain amount of debugging that's required. It may even seem that the buyer has to work twice as hard during the changeover time—especially if the manual and computerized systems are run in tandem for a while. But in the long run the extra effort and patience will be well worth it.

The buyer preparing for EDP should also practice analytical thinking, and try to visualize what it's going to be like working from statistical summaries rather than conventional memos and forms.

Under present systems, for example, you may expedite all open orders, depending on production control to tell you how critical each one is. Under an EDP system, what you'll probably get is a printout from the computer, listing either only delinquent orders, or showing all orders plus symbols for late or critical items. Although the EDP system itself will be much more efficient, it may take you a little while to get used to it. You'll have to learn the meanings of the various coding symbols, for one thing.

More specifically, there are at least five points the buyer should remember to get the most out of computerized purchasing methods:

1. It is extremely important that item descriptions within the EDP system be accurate and complete. In many cases, these descriptions are recorded on "mechanized" traveling requisitions: either edge-punched cards, tape, or tab cards. Then, as orders are prepared on semi-automatic typewriters, the data is captured for analysis within the computer.

This means that it's the buyer's responsibility to prepare accurate item descriptions of all his commodities right at the start. Without such exact descriptions, suppliers may not know what to ship. The whole point of the system will be defeated.

2. The buyer must assist in commodity coding, so that the computer can provide meaningful analyses of purchases by commodity group.

The danger here is that the buyer—when he's asked how many codes his commodities will require—may go off the deep end. He may feel that each of his major commodities requires all sorts of codes, sub-codes, and sub-sub-codes.

It's better to resist this tendency (which may be due to a subconscious wish to demonstrate the importance or complexity of the buyer's products). Commodity codes should be as broad as possible. And, if the buyer gives serious thought to the matter, he should be able to come up with just a few codes that will accurately reflect his buying patterns.

3. Once the commodity codes for an EDP system have been established, the buyer must be scrupulous in coding his orders into the proper categories. If he's at all slipshod in coding, the data that the computer furnishes simply won't be accurate.

It takes time to get a coding system working smoothly, and it requires a great deal of effort by individual buyers. But with practice the buyer can learn the consistency that's required for this part of a computer system.

In addition, if he has kept his commodity codes as broad as possible—as recommended in point 2 above—the actual coding operations will be that much easier for the buyer.

4. The buyer must remember to notify the computer whenever he takes any action regarding an order: changing quantities, prices, delivery dates, etc. The computer knows only what it's told, and if it's not kept up to date, its programmed actions will be meaningless.

Suppose that a computer is programmed to print out expediting letters on delinquent orders. If buyers give suppliers verbal okays to delay delivery dates, and then don't notify the computer of these okays, the machine will assiduously follow up orders that don't really need expediting.

Or if a buyer neglects to tell the computer that he and the supplier are considering a 100-part order complete when 99 items have arrived, the order will remain open until hell freezes over as far as the computer is concerned.

Best bet, therefore, is to think of the computer as similar to those freaks known to psychologists as *idiots savants:* unfortunates who can add countless numbers in their heads, or memorize pages at a glance—but who have trouble tying their own shoelaces.

5. The buyer working with a computerized purchasing system should constantly seek ways to make that system more efficient. As the one on the firing line, he's in an ideal position to spot possible improvements. He can tell what data he needs to do a better buying job, and he knows when he needs it and what the best format would be.

In negotiating an annual contract on an active commodity, for example, the buyer may want to know the total dollars that he has spent for the item in the last year. He may also want to know the frequency and volume of individual orders—and he may well want to have this data in a format that he can present to the potential vendor without editing.

If the buyer passes suggestions like these along to those responsible for over-all EDP planning, he'll be doing himself and his company a tremendous service.

40

PURCHASING BY OBJECTIVE

"Management by objective" has gotten a lot of publicity in recent years. It is currently one of the most popular methods for controlling the direction and thrust of any organization. And rightly so, because it's successful. When the top management of any enterprise clearly establishes over-all goals—and assigns specific goals to the various groups under it—there's much less chance of confusion. Each department and individual knows where it or he is going. There's no inadvertent working at cross purposes.

In addition, management by objective fosters strong motivation in those working under such a plan, and makes it easy to measure individual and departmental performance.

Right now, in purchasing departments across the country, thousands of buyers are working under management by objective programs. The top management of these firms have framed over-all goals for their companies, and have assigned specific goals to the purchasing department. The purchasing managers, in turn, have parceled out specific objectives for each of the buyers.

If you're working in such a firm, you have probably participated in setting your own current goals. The objectives may be part of an annual report—either from you to your boss, or from him to his boss. You're undoubtedly keeping track of your progress toward your objectives, so your performance can realistically be assessed.

Even if you aren't in such a situation you can still frame a set of goals for yourself, to make management by objective purchasing by objective.

While the best time to start such a program is at the beginning of a new year, there's no reason why you can't get going right now. All you have to do is draw up a list of the ways in which you can become a better buyer, and set yourself a target date.

In making the list, remember that you have to be specific. The objectives you set yourself must be expressed in quantitative form, so that you can later determine how well you've met them. Moreover, they should be realistic: not too high and not too low; attainable but not too easy to achieve.

Here's a list of 25 possible objectives that you might want to set yourself—but in each case it's up to you to fill in the blank space with whatever figure seems appropriate:

1. Reduce purchase costs of your commodities by __% or $__.
2. Add __ new suppliers to the approved bidders' list.
3. Eliminate __ sole-source situations.
4. Increase inventory turnover to __ times per year.
5. Improve suppliers' quality performance by __%.
6. Improve suppliers' delivery performance by __%.
7. Improve suppliers' cost-reduction contributions to $__.
8. Reduce average requisition-processing time to __ days.
9. Increase number of quality-certified suppliers to __.
10. Reduce number of requisitions with insufficient lead time by __%.
11. Reduce number of requisitions with other errors by __%.
12. Review __ commodities to determine feasibility of long-term contracts.
13. Review __ long-term contracts to determine their need and practicality.
14. Review standards list and reduce number of items to __.
15. Reduce average time per interview to __ minutes.
16. Make an in-depth market study of __ commodities.
17. Experiment with __ management techniques such as PERT/CPM, learning curves, price/cost analysis, etc.

18. Reduce the number of unplaced requisitions in your desk to __.
19. Explore the use of __ new materials or processes.
20. Visit __ vendors' plants.
21. Reduce number of back-door buys by __%.
22. Set up __ conferences between salesmen and operating departments.
23. Attend __ technically oriented trade shows.
24. Participate in __ purchasing workshops or seminars.
25. Read __ books on purchasing or allied business subjects.

This is a fairly long list of possible objectives, and some of these goals may not be particularly appropriate for you or for your company. On the other hand, there may be other objectives you'd like to add to the list. If so, get together with your boss and ask his assistance in developing what you and he think are fair and equitable goals for you as a buyer.

As a matter of fact, it's a good idea to get together with your boss even if you're extracting some of the goals listed above more or less verbatim. It's true that the objectives listed are all aimed at improving purchasing in general. But, because your boss is one echelon closer to top management, he has a better understanding of what the company's overall objectives currently are. He can therefore give you a better fix on what your goals should be. He can advise you on what's most important to your company, and where you should place the most emphasis in buying by objective.

Don't be misled into thinking that your company's objective can be expressed simply as "making money." While this is the ultimate objective of any profit-making enterprise, changing conditions often force a firm to reorder its priorities in establishing tactics to reach that objective. This is what management by objective is all about. When the company president tells his immediate aides what the over-all objective is, he doesn't just say, "Make money." Instead, he tells all the group leaders reporting to him *how* the company intends to make money.

These changes and shifts in corporate objectives often have an impact down at the buyer's level—and the buyer should consider them when he establishes his own goals.

For example, a firm may be faced with a situation where its image as a reliable firm needs brightening up. There has to be a concerted effort to improve the public relations image and restore confidence in the company: on the part of customers, stockholders, and the public at large.

For the buyer, this might mean stressing the quality of the goods he buys—making sure that suppliers deliver top-quality components so there won't be any product failures in the field. Improving vendors' quality performance would therefore become the over-riding goal for the buyer; there would be less emphasis on matters such as suppliers' cost reduction contributions. Also, as part of an over-all campaign to improve the company's public relations image, the buyer might want to add a new goal to his list: shift a specific percentage of his business to local sources near his firm's manufacturing facilities.

Another instance would be the situation where a firm is undertaking a diversification program. For the buyer, this would mean greater emphasis on finding new sources and exploring new processes. The broadening and expanding product line would demand this kind of action.

Or suppose that a company suddenly realizes that while it has a highly trained and competent staff heading its various operating groups, it is weak in back-up support. There aren't too many number two men who are ready to step into the breach if the top man moves up, out or over. This would be an especially critical situation if many of the top managers were approaching retirement. Quite likely, top management might call for stepped up training of executive replacements in all groups.

If this were to happen, it would mean extra emphasis on the buyer's personal development goals: numbers 23, 24 and 25 on the list given earlier in this chapter.

If you keep your goals specific, realistic and keyed to your company's current goals, purchasing by objective will become buying by perspective. And that's what good purchasing depends on.

41

MATERIALS MANAGEMENT AND THE BUYER

If you're a buyer working in a purchasing department organized along conventional lines, you may have wondered what it would be like to handle your buying job under a materials management set-up. You've probably read about MM's growing popularity as an organizational form. You many have pondered questions like the following:

"Does materials management mean anything to the buyer, or is its impact felt primarily at the purchasing agent's or director's level?"

"Are there special problems or opportunities presented to a buyer under a materials management set-up?"

"Are there any specific steps I could take to prepare for materials management, if my company decided to switch to such a set-up?"

Although these are perfectly legitimate questions, there aren't any textbook answers to them. The reason is that materials management itself—although it's a clearly defined concept—takes many shapes and forms. Different companies practice materials management to different degrees. There are also differences in the ways materials management has come about in various firms. No MM set-up, therefore, is exactly like any other.

To understand this more fully, consider the purpose and general philosophy of materials management as an organizational discipline. Quite simply, the classic purpose of materials management is to pull together all the various company functions associated with materials, and to give over-all responsibility for these functions to one individual. In a complete MM arrangement, the functions would be these:

(a) Purchasing
(b) Production control
(c) Inventory control
(d) Materials handling
(e) Traffic
(f) Physical distribution

In a complete materials management set-up, moreover, the functions listed above are all-inclusive. Inventory control, for example, means not simply the control of purchased goods such as raw materials, fabricated parts and subcontracted assemblies. It also includes work-in-process and finished goods stock control. In the area of physical distribution, complete materials management means the full responsibility for locating warehouses, laying them out, equipping them and staffing them.

Under such a set-up, if the top materials man is a good manager, jurisdictional rivalries tend to disappear or be minimized. Decisions relating to materials are made with a view to the over-all impact on all groups associated with material problems. Each division head has a common court of last resort—the materials manager—and the result is usually greater coordination and cooperation within the materials department itself.

Purchasing and production control, for example, can work more closely than ever on matters such as determining economic order quantities, taking advantage of volume price breaks, and paring safety stocks to realistic levels. Purchasing can also work more closely with materials handling specialists, to get advice on how suppliers' packing and shipping methods can be adapted to fit internal materials flow systems. It's for reasons such as these—and also because EDP is making it relatively easy to combine and analyze information from the various groups that make up the materials function—that materials management is growing in popularity.

But—and this is a most important point—it is also possible for a firm to practice materials management in fact but not in theory. This often happens when the purchasing agent or purchasing manager is given additional duties such as production control, inventory control, or traffic. In such a case the P.A. becomes a quasi-materials manager. A buyer working for him enjoys many of the major benefits of MM regardless of titles or organizational charts. And, if the P.A. delegates more and more of his purchasing responsibilities to the buyer (to give himself more time for broader-scope activities) the buyer in turn may become a *de facto* purchasing agent.

To get a true fix on what materials management might mean to him, a buyer should ask himself a series of questions. Each question should be designed to analyze specific situations within the buyer's firm. Here are some examples:

Are we already practicing materials management in fact if not on paper? If we are, is there a chance that this arrangement will be formalized? Am I a possible candidate for the purchasing agent's post if the P.A. moves up to materials manager?

If all the groups involved with materials are currently separate on the organizational chart, is there a chance that this will change? More importantly, how will the change probably come about? Will it evolve gradually, as the P.A. assumes additional responsibilities? Or will it be the result of a management edict forcing wholesale and sudden shifting of responsibilities? (If it's the latter, management will undoubtedly expect faster results from the new set-up.)

Who will head up the materials department as materials manager? The purchasing agent? The production control manager? Or will someone from another department—or even a complete newcomer to the company—be brought in to take over? (If the P.A. becomes materials manager, it's good news for the buyer even if someone else is shifted into the top purchasing slot. Reason: it's always helpful to have your top boss familiar with your duties and problems. But if the production manager or someone else is elevated to the materials manager's job, the buyer and everyone else in the department may have to re-sell some of purchasing's basic philosophies.)

To what level will the materials manager report? What other functions or departments will be on his organizational level? (This is important because formation of a materials department often upgrades the position of the materials head. He may be on a par with the managers of engineering, manufacturing, finance, sales, etc. This can help the buyer immeasurably in matters such as value analysis and value engineering.)

What functions will be included in the materials management set-up? Were these functions once clearly defined as the responsibilities of other departments? (If they were, there may be some initial resentment on the part of those formerly responsible for them. Manufacturing may feel that production control should still be under its domain; marketing may feel the same way about finished goods inventory control; etc. In working under a new materials management arrangement, no buyer can afford to ignore such highly personal reactions.)

From the above, it should be obvious that the buyer's role in materials management will depend to a great degree on the type, form and extent of the MM set-up. In some cases a switch to materials management may give the buyer more opportunities to develop broader knowledge. This would be especially true if the materials manager set up an internship program under which his staff could rotate assignments from time to time. Under such a program, the buyer might spend short periods working at other materials responsibilities—learning about production control, inventory control, traffic, etc.

In other cases a change to materials management may simply mean that the buyer has more opportunities to coordinate his purchasing duties with other functions. But, whether MM is formal or informal, complete or only partial in its scope, it's still up to the buyer to make the most of MM's advantages.

42

WHAT MAKES A GOOD BUYER?

One of the more bizarre definitions of purchasing agents—and hence, by implication, of anyone whose profession is buying—runs like this:

"The typical purchasing agent is a man past middle life, spare, wrinkled, bald, intelligent, passive, cold, non-committal; with eyes like a codfish, polite in contact, but at the same time unresponsive, cool, calm, and damnably composed as a concrete post or plaster of Paris cast; a human petrification with a heart of feldspar and without charm or the friendly germ; minus bowels, passions, or sense of humor. Happily they never reproduce, and all of them finally go to Hell."

This definition (commonly attributed to Elbert Hubbard) goes back at least to the early 1900's. If nothing else, it's obviously dated. But, without commenting further on its accuracy or objectivity, let's try a little experiment. Let's reverse all the attributes in the original definition, to see if this produces a more up-to-date, realistic and attractive portrait of those whose business is buying.

Subjected to such a reverse-English twist, the re-definition might read something like this:

"The typical purchasing agent (or buyer) is a man not yet mature, fat, smooth, hairy, stupid, impatient, hot-tempered, partisan; with eyes like a fox, impolite in contact and quick with answers, tepid, excitable, and with the composure of a bowl of Jello or cornmeal mush; an inhuman blob with a marshmallow heart and full of charm and unfriendly germs; with lots of guts, emotions and smiles. They are all sex maniacs, and all of them finally go to heaven."

This re-definition (admittedly a bit unfair in its use of antonyms) is just about as repellent as the original one. Nor is it any more accurate. But the experiment does prove a point that's important in any consideration of what makes a good buyer: the buying job is one that demands a balanced combination of many personal attributes, rather than over-emphasis on one or two outstanding characteristics.

A good buyer, in other words, has the enthusiasm and zeal of a good salesman: one who's completely sold on his own product line and on what it can offer customers. But, at the same time, the buyer's enthusiasm is tempered by a healthy skepticism. He knows that much of any salesman's fervor stems from the nature of the sales-oriented personality. He realizes that much of the sales patter he's subjected to every day has to be discounted accordingly.

A good buyer also has a sound technical understanding of the commodities he's responsible for—without the engineering-type tunnel vision that often results in over-specification.

In addition, a good buyer is one who's attentive to detail—without getting lost in pointless nit-picking, or in clerical make-work.

By the same token, a good buyer is inquisitive, inquiring and imaginative—but his questioning attitude is always pragmatic. He's interested in results rather than in theories. He's a clinician rather than a pedant.

What it boils down to is the fact that measuring purchasing performance (determining what makes a good buyer) is an extremely tough proposition. The buying job is so diverse, and demands so many skills and attributes, that it's difficult to come up with absolute guidelines or benchmarks.

This becomes plainly evident when you try to apply conventional performance measurement techniques to the buying job. Under such appraisal methods, there are basically two factors that have to be considered: quantity of the work, and quality of the work.

For routine and simple jobs, these two factors add up to just about a complete assessment of over-all performance. A ditch-digger moves so many cubic yards of earth a day, and he digs either a good ditch or a poor one: one that's straight, true and well-shored, or one that collapses two minutes after he climbs out of it. And, in any office, it's easy to run similar output/accuracy checks on typists, file clerks, invoice-approvers and others in clerical positions.

But when you try to measure either the quantity or quality of a buyer's work, you immediately face some rather sticky questions.

In the first place, how do you measure quantity of the output at any buyer's desk? Is it number of purchase orders placed? Of requisitions received? Of individual line items? Quotations issued? Dollar volume?

The basic trouble with using any of these factors as work-measurement standards is that they are to a large extent beyond the buyer's control. He can't work any more productively than his commodity assignments dictate. Moreover, many of these factors actually give false indications of a buyer's efficiency. Suppose that a buyer manages to reduce his purchase order count through blanket orders, other long-term agreements, and better coordination with production control. While such action would be highly desirable, it would show up as a debit against the buyer if purchase order volume were considered an absolute measure of efficiency.

In the second place, it's equally difficult to assess the quality of a buyer's work. Is quality to be measured as accuracy—reflected in the number of change notices that a buyer has to issue to correct his original orders? This isn't fair because many external forces have an impact on pending orders: industry-wide price changes, modification of in-plant production requirements, etc. Again, these are matters beyond the buyer's control. Nor is it fair, really, to measure a buyer's work-quality in terms of cost reductions. Some commodities naturally lend themselves more readily to cost reduction efforts than others.

Does this mean that determining what makes a good buyer, and measuring individual performance, is impossible? Not really. But it does mean that any consideration of this matter requires a great deal of judgment. In considering the following list of 25 points, for example, both a buyer and his supervisor should realize that yes-no answers probably won't apply.

With this proviso in mind, it's fairly safe to say that a good buyer is one who:

1. Handles his fair share of the departmental workload.
2. Performs his work quickly and accurately.
3. Lets his boss know if his workload could be increased without compromising its quality.

4. Pitches in to help other buyers (or expediters, or clerks) when necessary.

5. Accepts overtime work, with or without pay, as required.

6. Doesn't gripe if his commodity assignments are switched.

7. Has a system for keeping his pending work organized in his desk.

8. Sees to it that his fellow buyers know his work-organizing system.

9. Arrives at the office on time, and doesn't jump the gun at closing time.

10. Offers workable ideas for improving purchasing systems.

11. Knows his vendors' capabilities and shortcomings.

12. Understands that his suppliers' performance reflects his own performance.

13. Keeps up with technological and market developments in his field.

14. Is completely familiar with his company's product line.

15. Continually adds to his knowledge of business law and related subjects.

16. Works within the procedures and policy guidelines established by the head of purchasing.

17. Maintains high standards of dress and decorum.

18. Can justify his decisions on awarding business in specific rather than general terms.

19. Knows how to challenge specifications and delivery dates without appearing defiant.

20. Accepts constructive criticism without griping or specious excuses.

21. Takes the long-term view in developing supplier relationships.

22. Recognizes that any company—his own and vendors'—is made up of human beings.

23. Is never arrogant.

24. Enjoys his work.

25. Is loyal to his immediate boss, to the purchasing department, and to his company.

43

THE PRACTICAL SIDE OF ETHICS

Of all the intangible factors that have a bearing on a buyer's success or failure in the purchasing profession, a strong sense of ethics is undoubtedly the most important. It just isn't true that "nice guys finish last." The buyer who develops a strong code of ethical conduct will simultaneously build a personal reputation for honesty and integrity. This reputation will be one of the most valuable assets of his career. It will follow him wherever he goes.

A good reputation, of course, is essential in any walk of life or profession. But the need for good ethics is especially important to buyers. The reason is that the buying job involves a great deal of power, and there are therefore more opportunities for power to be abused.

The buyer's power stems from the fact that he is the one who determines how business is to be awarded among suppliers. The decisions that he makes have powerful and far-reaching results. They affect individual salesmen's commissions, sales managers' performance records, corporate profit structures—even a firm's ability to survive in the competitive marketplace.

Against this background, it would be naive to suggest that the buyer doesn't wield considerable power and authority—and that he couldn't, if he wanted to, use his position for personal ends. The opportunities will always be there: for kick-backs, excessive entertainment or gifts, personal purchases at reduced prices, etc. And it's solely up to the buyer as to whether or not he takes advantage of these opportunities, because most of them can't be controlled by procedural rules or auditing safeguards. (Even under sealed-bid procedures, there will always be opportunities for the buyer to favor one supplier over another—in developing bidders' lists, making comments on vendor performance, etc.)

Whether or not a buyer takes advantage of his position, then, will ultimately depend on his own personal integrity. He will either be honest —or he won't. And, in the final analysis, nothing he reads in this book or any other will have the slightest effect in this regard.

But—and this is an important point—true ethics isn't just a simple matter of honesty *vs* dishonesty. In the business world, ethics is a broad, complex subject. It reflects a professional as well as a personal life-style. It puts the buyer under an obligation to play 100% fair with suppliers in his official capacity, and not to take undue advantage of his position even on behalf of his company.

Some buyers may find it difficult to understand this. They may feel (and not without reason) that many salesmen and other marketing specialists are less than completely ethical in their sales approaches. And they may reason that this frees them of the obligation to follow strict ethical rules in handling their jobs, because their jobs basically involve counter-strategies to meet sellers' tactics.

To put it in another way, such buyers may feel that since "caveat emptor" ("let the buyer beware") has become a recognized part of the language, there's no reason why "caveat venditor" ("let the seller beware") shouldn't apply with equal force.

As a result, some buyers may from time to time be tempted to misuse the power inherent in their position by:

— Misrepresenting their companies' requirements;
— Divulging information on competitive prices;
— Making unauthorized use of confidential technical information.

Although the short-term results of such actions may work to the buying company's advantage, they don't pay off in the long run. From a practical as well as a moral viewpoint, good ethics are simply good business. To understand this, let's take a look at each of the situations noted above, to see what eventually happens when a buyer plays fast and loose with his sense of ethics.

There are, for example, two ways in which a buyer can misrepresent his firm's quantity requirements for purchased goods. In setting up blanket orders or annual contracts, he can inflate the estimates of annual usage. Or, in negotiating one-time orders, he can imply that the first order is a trial order, to be followed by other orders for much larger quantities.

If the supplier takes the quantity requirements given him at face value, he may indeed lower his prices. But what happens when the high-volume business doesn't materialize? Under many blanket order agreements, the buyer and his company may face back-charges for failure to hit estimated volume. And, if a supplier accepts a one-time order at a low price because he visualizes future high-volume business that doesn't materialize, he'll naturally be out to recoup his losses next time around. Moreover, if his acceptance of the first order has involved tooling set-ups, he'll be in an excellent position to make the buyer pay extra for requirements that *do* arise in the future.

Divulging information on competitive bids—either through strongly worded hints, or "accidental" disclosure of bid forms, letters or other documents—is another practice that will eventually boomerang and work to the disadvantage of the buying company.

It's true that a supplier getting this kind of preferential treatment may lower his prices more than he otherwise would have. The buyer gets a better price, and his company's costs are less than they might have been. But the important point is that the whole concept of competitive bidding is weakened. The "favored" supplier knows that he was given a break. He may wonder how many other suppliers were given similar opportunities. And he'll certainly be less likely to submit his best bid first on future requirements.

Long-term, in fact, a buyer who's known as a "price-shopper" might just as well be known as an "auctioneer." From a practical viewpoint, his ability to buy aggressively for his company will be just about nil.

It's equally hazardous, from a long-term practical viewpoint, to be less than scrupulous about keeping suppliers' technical information confidential. Just as buyers depend on suppliers to provide new ideas, suppliers depend on buyers to honor the confidentiality of the ideas they come up with. Quite simply, it is a matter of trust.

What happens when a buyer violates this trust—perhaps by divulging one supplier's design ideas to another supplier whose basic pricing structure is more favorable to the buying company? The answer is equally simple: the first company stops coming up with ideas. It may take a little while for it to get the message; there may be more than one occasion for the buyer to get away with such fancy footwork—but the end result will eventually be a complete drying up of new ideas and concepts from all suppliers. (The firms that are discriminated against won't want to come up with suggestions; the ones getting the advantage of the discrimination will feel that they don't have to.)

In the long run, then, a strict code of ethical conduct will do far more than give the buyer a comfortable sense of personal satisfaction. It will also help him to do the very best job in the position he's been hired to fill.

44

MANAGEMENT SKILLS
BRING MANAGEMENT STATUS

What's the difference between a purchasing manager and a buyer? It's precisely the same difference that exists between an accounting manager and an accountant, a sales manager and a salesman, an engineering manager and an engineer—or between any other department head and his professional staff.

A manager, by definition, is one who directs and guides the work of others, to accomplish whatever over-all results are desired. He is the one who is ultimately responsible for the total performance of his group. In a very real sense, he *is* the group, or department, or division.

If you're a typical buyer, you'd probably like to move up to a managerial position. Perhaps you know that this may involve several steps: from buyer to senior buyer to supervisory buyer or section head—or through whatever organizational routes are applicable in your firm. But chances are, no matter how many steps it may take, you'd eventually like to become purchasing manager. You know that the rewards are greater—both in terms of financial compensation and personal satisfaction—at the higher levels of any organization.

If you do feel this way, there are specific steps you can take to reach your goal.

Step one, of course, should be to mount an educational program incorporating every training aid possible: university extension or correspondence courses in management subjects, workshops, seminars, and as much reading as you can possibly pack in. It's true that you'll look in vain for any text titled "How to Become a Purchasing Manager in Three Easy Lessons." But there are countless books and periodicals on general management subjects that you can profitably read to get an insight into the art and science of executive leadership.

As you read up on the subject, you'll undoubtedly come across a wide variety of recommended approaches: management by results, management by objective, theory X *vs* theory Y management, etc. But when you sift it all out, you'll probably recognize that good management practices can really be summed up in a not-too-long list. Based on your own experiences in the past, with good and not-so-good bosses, you may want to develop your own list. If you do, it will probably look something like the following:

A good manager is one who:

1. Skillfully interprets corporate policies.
2. Establishes departmental policies consistent with those of the company.
3. Sets procedures to implement policies.
4. Handles many projects simultaneously.
5. Keeps perspective in assigning priorities to projects.
6. Establishes the department's operating budget.
7. Apportions his staff's workloads.
8. Assesses his staff's performance.
9. Determines the amount of supervision each staffer requires.
10. Rewards good performance, through promotions or salary increases.
11. Includes suggestions for improvement with rebukes for poor work.
12. Trains and develops his staff.
13. Recruits new personnel as necessary.
14. Backs his staffers to the limit when he knows they're right.
15. Is willing to try new management techniques.

As you look at this list, one point should be very clear: there are many management skills that you're already responsible for, as a buyer. The very nature of your job forces you to work with people, both inside and outside the company, and that is what management is all about. Here's a point-by-point rundown:

Interpreting policies: As a buyer, you have to interpret the purchasing policies that have been established by the head of your department. You have to be sure that you understand them yourself—and you also have to be able to translate them for suppliers in specific terms.

Establishing policies: This is one area where your buying duties don't involve direct participation. But there will be many instances where your counsel and advice can be of benefit to the one who does set policy.

Setting procedures: Every buying position, with whatever commodity assignments are involved, is a microcosm of a larger organization. To make things work smoothly and efficiently at your own desk, you have undoubtedly devised special work-flow techniques and systems.

Handling many projects: If you're a typical buyer, you're undoubtedly well versed in juggling a multiplicity of regular assignments, special projects, etc.

Maintaining perspective: Another point that really doesn't need elaboration. If a buyer can't assign realistic priorities to his many activities, he won't survive for long.

Establishing budgets: You may not have a direct voice in allocating departmental funds for salaries, travel, supplies, etc. On the other hand, your inputs on material costs are probably a prime factor for operating departments' material budgets.

Apportioning workloads: This is something you do every day, in distributing orders to those suppliers who are currently in the best position to handle your business.

Assessing performance: Another routine matter for buyers—who have to determine which suppliers are qualified to take care of their firms' requirements.

Determining what supervision is needed: If all suppliers were equally capable and had exactly the same equipment, this is an area you wouldn't get into in your buying job. But in real life it doesn't work out that way. You're constantly involved in situations where one supplier has to be watched a bit more closely than another—whether on delivery, quality, or any other aspect of his over-all performance.

Rewarding good performance: Again, this is something you do every day as a buyer. The good suppliers get the business, and they also get a chance at more business as it materializes.

Penalizing poor performance: The main penalty you exact as a buyer is not to award future orders. But chances are you also try to help those suppliers whose performance isn't up to par, by suggesting ways in which they can improve.

Training and development: For all suppliers, you're probably working out ways in which they can boost performance, take over new and broader responsibilities, etc.

Recruitment: No matter how satisfied you are with your present corps of suppliers, you're probably seeking to expand it for even greater flexibility.

Whole-hearted support: As a buyer, you are the number one in-plant representative of the suppliers that serve your firm. If you back them up 100% when you know they're right, you're living up to what is essentially a management responsibility.

Trying new techniques: Have you ever used PERT/CPM approaches in monitoring special projects, or in expediting suppliers' progress on big jobs? Or have you used learning curves or cost/price analysis in negotiations with suppliers? If you have, you have already had practical experience in management science.

In a very real sense, then, you are already a manager. You can add to your management skills by constant practice in your daily activities—with particular emphasis on those where you feel you need extra development.

As you do this, you will polish up all your skills, and you will also demonstrate that you are doing so. Nothing succeeds like success, and the buyer's job is essentially a highly "visible" one. The opportunities and challenges in the purchasing field are almost endless, and the transition from buyer to purchasing manager is one that's made every day. With perseverance, planning and a lot of hard work, you can make it too.

INDEX